Wisdom from the Garden . . .

"I learned from Daddy to garden very early in the morning, shortly after sunrise. He claims it's to take advantage of the coolest part of the day, but I've always suspected other reasons harder to explain. Who could resist seeing sunrise sprinkle golden light over the garden and give birth to a new day?"

"Flowers go in and out of fashion. For many people like me who gardened with parents and grandparents, old-fashioned flowers like zinnias, marigolds, and snapdragons bring back deep remembrances of loved ones. I know from personal experience that flowers—with their scent and color—are powerful sources of memories. I can't imagine a garden without these old friends!"

"As much as I love to look out at my fading roses, willowy purple delphiniums, and the delicacy of pink astilbes, I know they aren't the real reason I garden. The inner peace and joy that have come to fill my life are the true fruits of my labor."

"As the garden becomes a dearer and dearer friend, I've learned that true respect for life is without boundaries. The garden deserves as much of my heart in winter, when its energy has descended to its roots, as in the summer, when roses and lilies are blooming."

Also by Nancy Hutchens

Memories of a Midwestern Farm

Published by POCKET BOOKS

A
Garden's Grace

Down-to-Earth
Lessons and
Simple Rewards

Nancy Hutchens

Illustrated by Richard Lang Chandler

Pocket Books
New York   London   Toronto   Sydney   Tokyo   Singapore

Two lines from "To My American Gardener, with Love" from *Poems & Sketches of E. B.
White*. Copyright © 1981 by E. B. White. Reprinted by permission of HarperCollins
Publishers, Inc.

"Come On into My Tropical Garden" reproduced with permission of Curtis Brown Ltd,
London, on behalf of Grace Nichols. Copyright © 1988 by Grace Nichols.

Poem on page 169 from *The Spirit of Tao* translated and edited by Thomas Cleary, © 1991,
1993. Reprinted by arrangement with Shambhala Publications, Inc., 300 Massachusetts
Avenue, Boston, MA 02115.

An *Original* Publication of POCKET BOOKS

POCKET BOOKS, a division of Simon & Schuster Inc.
1230 Avenue of the Americas, New York, NY 10020

Copyright © 1997 by Nancy Hutchens

Library of Congress Cataloging-in-Publication Data

Hutchens, Nancy.
    A garden's grace: down to earth lessons and simple rewards /
Nancy Hutchens; illustrated by Richard Long Chandler.
        p.   cm.
    Includes index.
    ISBN: 0-671-56849-3
    1. Gardening.   2. Gardening—Hudson River Valley (N.Y. and N.J.)
3. Nature craft.   4. Hutchens, Nancy.   I. Title.
SB455.H84   1997
635.9—dc21   96-29499
                                                              CIP

First Pocket Books trade paperback printing April 1997

10   9   8   7   6   5   4   3   2   1

POCKET and colophon are registered trademarks of Simon & Schuster Inc.

Cover design and front cover art by Richard Chandler

Interior design by Barbara Cohen Aronica

Printed in the U.S.A.

To Joseph Wilbur Hutchens
for passing on his love of seeing things grow

Flowers respond to something in the gardener's face—
Some secret in the heart, some special grace.

—E. B. White,
"To My American Gardener, with Love"

Acknowledgments

I'm indebted to many people for their contribution to this book and making the solitary job of writing more sociable. Janis Vallely, my agent, mentor, and friend, generously used her finely tuned ear to help me when I was off key. Dick Chandler's exquisite illustrations bring my words and garden to life. Everyone at Pocket Books has been wonderful to work with—especially my editor, Amy Pierpont, whose enthusiasm and insight are boundless. Barbara Chandler and Sue Fox offered helpful suggestions and a friendly smile when I needed them most. My grandmother, Mamaw Tribby, died when I was sixteen, but she continues to inspire and guide me as a writer, a gardener, and a woman. My greatest satisfaction in writing this book is enabling others to hear her voice. Last and most importantly, I'm especially appreciative of Michael—my partner in all things—for never doubting me and sharing the journey.

Contents

SUMMER: THE FLOWERING

AUTUMN: THE BOUNTY

CHAPTER 7 ESSENTIAL TASKS 91

CHAPTER 8 IN DUE TIME 106

CHAPTER 9 THE JOURNEY HOME 122

WINTER: THE STILLNESS

Spring

The Promise

For lo, the winter is past, the rain is over and gone; the flowers appear on the earth; the time of the singing of birds is come, and the voice of the turtledove is heard in our land. . . .

—Song of Solomon

1

A Time of Renewal

In the morning the sun rose brilliant
and quickly melted the thin ice on the water, and
the warm air all around vibrated with the vapour given off
by the awakening earth. Last year's grass grew green again
and the young grass thrust up its tiny blades; the buds
swelled on the guelder-rose and the currant-bushes. . . .
Spring had really come.

—Leo Tolstoi, *Anna Karenina*

In gardening I've discovered a language that rekindles the joy of my childhood on the farm. Each spring when I was growing up Daddy knew the moment when nature had worked her magic and the ground was ready for planting. Life on the farm was guided by the rhythms of the seasons. Like our ancestors before us, we grew our own food for the body and flowers for the soul. Mother loved her deep pink peonies, tall blue-bearded irises, lilacs, and wild roses; and Daddy always planted sunflowers, zinnias, snapdragons, and morning glories in the kitchen garden. Both of my parents were busy keeping pace with Mother Nature, so it was my grandmother, Mamaw Tribby, who taught me most about gardening in the hours we spent tending her flowers. While we weeded and watered her beloved yellow roses, she talked about her flowers as if they were her truest, most faithful friends. She believed that gardening was not a hobby but an essential activity that renews the soul as surely as spring renews the earth.

I didn't have my own garden until I was almost thirty, but with every passing year it captures more of my heart. Despite many years of living in cities and suburbs, I've turned into a farmer, just like Daddy, my grandfathers, and their fathers before them. As I cultivate my own piece of earth dressed in old rubber boots and a threadbare flannel jacket, farming and gardening seem to be a part of the same ancient process of clearing the land, preparing the soil, and planting our sustenance. At work in my flower beds, I'm often surprised by tiny sensory impressions that summon memories of home and a way of life I left long ago. The vivid smells of springtime—pungent composted manure and sweet hyacinths—and sights like a field of yellow daffodils evoke those years with a clarity that words cannot express. When I clean out the soggy leaves that cradle my early daffodils, I can almost hear my Mamaw Tribby saying, "One of these days you'll move away from the farm, but in the spring when the daffodils return and the earth is young again you'll recall these times." She died many years ago, but when I'm in the garden her voice is still there by my side offering down-to-earth advice and reminding me of the simple happiness I've always found there.

Frost-locked all the winter,
Seeds, and roots, and stones of fruits, . . .

Swollen with sap put forth their shoots;
Curled-headed ferns sprout in the lane;
Birds sing and pair again.

There is no time like Spring,
When life's alive in everything.
      —Christina Rossetti, "Spring"

Wisdom from Mamaw Tribby's Garden

Once in a golden hour
I cast to earth a seed.
Up there came a flower,
The people said, a weed.
——Alfred Lord Tennyson,
"The Flower"

In the spring, flowers that sprout from stray seeds begin to pop up in the most unlikely places. I've found single coreopsis, coneflowers, impatiens, zinnias, marigolds, columbine, and many others scattered throughout the yard. These "volunteers" always bring a smile to my face when I remember how much Mamaw Tribby loved them. A stray flower never went without a home in her garden. When a volunteer appeared along the path in the backyard or beside the driveway, she stopped at that very moment to carefully mark it with a stone so no one would crush it. When the little volunteer was established enough to be transplanted, we would convert one of the large tin cans she had accumulated over the winter into a flowerpot. First, she punched drainage holes in the bottom, then filled it with two or three inches of gravel, and her recipe for potting soil—compost mixed with soil and a little builder's sand. If we didn't have any of this particular flower in the garden, it stayed on the porch in a place of honor perched beside the rows of begonias and geraniums. If it was a flower already growing in the garden, it rejoined its brothers and sisters.

One chilly spring day I remember accidentally crushing a tiny pansy volunteer. "We have lots of pansies on the other side of the house," I said when I saw the look on her face. She patiently explained, "Every little volunteer is a miracle that has proven what obstacles we can overcome. When we come along and give it a safe home in rich soil, I always feel like we're doing God's work."

Lessons
from the
Gardener's Journal

Becoming a Gardener

What makes a garden
And why do gardens grow?
Love lives in gardens—
God and lovers know!
    —Caroline Giltinan, "The Garden"

I set out my first garden shortly after I met and married my husband, Michael. We bought a weekend cottage in upstate New York and—without even thinking about it—I picked up a few impatiens and snap-dragons at a local farmer's market. Over the next ten years that tiny flower garden grew and grew as I rediscovered the joy of sinking my fingers into the earth. Then six years ago Michael and I moved into our cozy house on the Hudson River with its old village garden that dates back to the Revolution. Every day I spend time with my flowers, and as I watch them bloom and fade, I think about the grace I've gained from my beloved garden.

In looking at gardens over the years I've found that certain spots revive the spirit and elevate the mind, and to me these places are the true gardens—whether they are small or large, public or private. The love and devotion of the gardeners who created them and tend them every day is expressed in their very beauty. Many years ago I lived in a brand-new house where a professional landscaper did all of the gardening. Despite a breathtaking mountain location, I never felt a strong connection to the land. The earth and I didn't struggle to overcome droughts, floods, weeds, and the onslaught of pests—the everyday life of the garden. The garden had no history, no past. When the flower bed bloomed it was only a pretty sight, not one that my sweat, my aching back, and my heart had fostered. Becoming a gardener requires giving something of ourselves, but what better way is there to spend a life?

To create a little flower is the labour of the ages.
    —William Blake, "Proverbs of Hell"

The Beginning Steps

1. Decide on whether you want a bed (visible on all sides) or a border (up against a boundary) and where you want to put it. Check to see how much sun the location gets. A space with at least four to six hours of sun a day is the easiest way to get started. Check the soil. A simple soil tester available in nurseries will tell you if it's acidic or alkaline. If it sticks together in a clump, it may be clay. If so, drainage may be a problem. Is it sandy? In that case it may not hold water. Both conditions can be improved by adding a combination of compost, peat moss, and topsoil.

2. Plan your flower bed by drawing and labeling each plant on a piece of graph paper as well as fences, shrubs, walkways, and benches. Take plant height, color, and blooming time into consideration. Annuals, of course, bloom consistently all summer. In addition to annuals, seek out a few hearty, agreeable perennials. A good starter selection includes rudbeckia—yellow black-eyed Susans and its purple cousin, echinacea—as well as coreopsis, asters, sweet william, and pinks and a few herbs like basil, thyme, or dill.

3. Decide on the style you like—formal, cottage, Japanese, new American. A formal style has straight lines and symmetry. The cottage style is full, lush, and informal with no apparent design, but it's much harder than it looks. Japanese is the most difficult and requires subtlety and knowledge of unusual plants. The new American style strives for a natural look by using lower-maintenance native flowers.

4. Check the plant hardiness zone of your location. The United States is divided into eleven zones based upon average annual *minimum* temperature. Perennials and shrubs will survive the winter as long as the thermometer doesn't go below a specific temperature. The zone tells you that temperature, although it doesn't tell you how much heat

the plant will tolerate. Hardiness maps are readily available in nurseries and from nursery catalogs. The label of most plants (other than annuals) specifies the zones where they can be grown safely. Most nurseries only carry stock suitable for the local zone. A frost-free date is associated with each zone and represents the green light for planting annuals outside.

5. Buy peat moss, compost, and flower fertilizer and a good-quality spade, trowel, and gloves before you prepare your garden. Lay out your garden using a garden hose for a curved edge or string on stakes for a square.

6. Remove the sod to uncover the earth and pull weeds by the roots. If the soil is dry, dampen it slightly. Turn over the soil with a spade by digging about eight to ten inches deep. Prepare the soil by spreading compost two inches thick and working it in with the spade. If you have heavy clay soil, also add an inch of damp peat moss. Apply a flower fertilizer according to directions on the package. Power tillers—available for rental in most areas—can be used instead of a spade, but they only work the soil to a depth of six to eight inches. Avoid overdoing it with the power tiller and leaving the soil too crumbly. For best results, let the tilled bed sit six to eight weeks before you plant.

7. Purchase your flowers when you are ready to plant. Plant your new annuals after the frost-free date. Most perennials can be safely planted a few weeks earlier. Plant the flowers the depth suggested in the instructions. Create a massed effect by clustering several plants. I usually set flowers closer than suggested to crowd out weeds and create an overblown, cottage look. Water them well.

8. Spread a mulch such as pine bark on the soil to discourage weeds and retain moisture. Leave the base of the plant exposed to help prevent insects. Mulch the rest of the bed for a uniform and attractive look.

9. Weed, water, and feed as your flowers grow. Their needs aren't complicated, just specific. Understand them and they'll give you more pleasure than you can imagine.

Spring Tasks

> But each spring . . . a gardening instinct, sore as the
> sap rising in the trees, stirs within us. We look about
> and decide to tame another little bit of ground.
> —Lewis Gannett

I've always thought of March as the ugly month. The last traces of snow have vanished, exposing the full extent of winter's foul handiwork. As I look at the dead, moldy leaves knotted in hard-to-reach crevices, branches and twigs tossed around like toothpicks, mulch from borders bleeding into the lawn, my heart sinks thinking about all that needs to be done. Even the dried stems of sedum and rudbeckia—left in the garden for a sculptured effect—have disintegrated. Cheerful flashes of color from early-blooming crocus and snowdrops are a welcome sight but do little to alter the impact of last season's discards. My first venture outside is tentative as I get my "garden legs." Then I begin a serious survey of the damage and try to visualize the plans I've worked on over the winter. Soon I'm picking up the dead wood and clearing debris and wondering how I'll manage to get everything done on my spring "to do" list. Creating this list each winter has become an important and comforting ritual. I now know that preparing my list will not only make tackling spring cleanup less daunting, but will bring me ever closer to experiencing the delights of my garden for yet another year.

Spring "To Do" List

❧ Remove every bit of dead leaves and debris.

❧ Start seeds and begonia tubers indoors.

❧ As soon as the soil is crumbly, compost beds and plant early seeds such as sweet peas and lettuce.

❧ Divide overgrown perennials or those to be propagated.

❧ Prune rosebushes and other woody shrubs, vines, and fruit trees.

❧ Fill outdoor containers with pansies.

❧ Set up garden hoses and remove patio furniture from storage. If necessary, paint and make repairs.

❧ Plant flowering shrubs.

❧ Prepare new beds. Mulch and edge the beds and borders.

❧ Purchase new perennials from catalogs and garden centers and plant from mid-April through May.

❧ Purchase annuals and plant after the frost date.

❧ Fill container pots with plants overwintered in the house and buy new stock as needed, and move outside in early to mid-May, depending on the weather.

The Prettiest Pansy Salad

Take all the sweetness of a gift unsought,
And for the pansies send me back a thought.
—Sarah Dowdney

What could be more delightful than a fresh garden salad with the brightly colored faces of pansies tucked in its leaves. Like me, many gardeners have turned to the pansy to liven up bulbs in the spring and mums in the fall. Then we quickly fall in love with the outrageous colors and cat's-paw markings on this member of the violet family. This salad pairs pansies and Vidalia onions—two of spring's sweetest gifts. What an exquisite reward for a day's labor!

Use about eight cups of washed and shredded mixed salad greens such as red or green leaf lettuce and oak leaf lettuce. This salad should be made with delicate rather than bitter greens like radicchio and arugula. Add six small sprigs of fresh green herbs like oregano, chervil, thyme, basil, or dill, washed and chopped; one small whole piece of endive cut into thin slivers; and a small Vidalia onion, finely chopped. Mix all of the salad ingredients.

To make the dressing, whisk until well blended three quarters of a cup of high-quality, extra-virgin olive oil, one tablespoon of olive oil infused with basil, and one tablespoon of olive oil infused with garlic with a quarter cup of tarragon vinegar. Just before serving, pour the dressing over the salad and mix with your hands. You may want to reserve some of the dressing for later use. Serve on individual salad plates. Salt and sprinkle fresh ground pepper to taste. Dot each salad with five or six capers and decorate the plate with as many washed and drained pansies as you

like. Be sure the pansies weren't treated with pesticide. Pansies add a slightly sweet but peppery taste to the salad. Serves six. Try with grilled vegetables and a hot, crusty French bread.

Lilac Hand Tonic

This oil is a soothing tonic for the gardener's hands in the spring before they have toughened.

For an excellent hand or body massage oil: mix a quarter cup of cold-pressed almond oil, an eighth of a cup of the highest quality extra-virgin cold-pressed olive oil, a quarter teaspoon of eucalyptus and lavender essence each. Add about ten drops of lilac oil or to suit. Store in a decorative bottle and cork. Keeps for two to three months.

> Who thought of the lilac? "I," dew said,
> "I made the lilac out of my head."
> "She made the lilac? Pooh!" trilled a linnet,
> And each dew-note had a lilac in it.
> —Humbert Wolfe, "The Lilac"

2

An Honest Day's Work

Write it down that here I labored
   Here I sang and laughed and neighbored.
That this yard should glow with beauty
   Spurred my lagging soul to duty.
That there should be splendor here
   Kept me toiling year by year.
Here in phlox, tulip and marigold
   Were my every purpose told.
Every thought and every act
   Was to keep this home intact.
                    —Mamaw Tribby, 1952

As much as I enjoy looking out my window at fading roses, willowy purple delphiniums, and the delicacy of pink astilbes, I know that they are not the real reason I garden. The inner peace and joy that fill my life are the true fruits of my labor. Although work has always been important to me, it was through gardening that I discovered it can be a powerful spiritual teacher. The most important lesson I've learned from gardening has been to devote myself completely to whatever I'm doing, but my efforts must spring from love.

About fifteen years ago I was living and working in midtown Manhattan, surrounded by skyscrapers and subways and feeling a long way from the farm. Work seemed to consume my whole life. I wanted to show everyone—including myself—that I could succeed, and the weight of the world seemed to be on my shoulders. Then, shortly after Michael and I bought a little weekend cottage in upstate New York and broke ground for my first flower bed, a magical pathway began to unfold.

This discovery led out my kitchen door and into my own backyard. I stayed put for many years, continuing to live in the same part of the city, doing the same work, but my weekends were now filled with gardening. I began to think of flowers as the shape of love. Gardening was something I did for myself—solely to bring love into the world. Worries were forgotten as I became absorbed in the endless stream of simple tasks involved in raising flowers. Although I've always been a busy person with a million things on my mind, I soon found that an inner silence surrounded me when I was in the garden. Often I lost all sense of time, and the five minutes I was going to spend staking delphiniums or deadheading roses stretched into an hour.

In the spring when there is so much to do, it's tempting to jump into everything at once like a whirling dervish. Instead, I take a deep breath, step back, and think to myself, "First things first. I can't do it all overnight." On the farm Daddy constantly reminded my brothers and me of the importance of keeping our minds focused on the job. He would say, "If you're not thinking about what you're doing, you're not giving it your best." I quickly learned the damage I could do to my beloved flowers when I let my mind wander—the perennial uprooted accidentally, the newly sprouted dahlia broken when I didn't watch my step, the rosebud cut when the pruning shears slipped.

Through gardening I've learned to give myself completely to whatever I'm doing—whether it's baking bread, planting a rose, or writing a book—and let my heart be my guide so that every moment is a joy, regardless of the outcome.

Yes, in the poor man's garden grow
Far more than herbs and flowers—
Kind thoughts, contentment, peace of mind,
And joy for weary hours.
    —Mary Howitt, "The Poor Man's Garden"

Wisdom from Mamaw Tribby's Garden

To labor is to pray.
    —ancient motto of Benedictine monks

Mamaw Tribby taught me that the true secret of becoming a gardener is finding joy in the process of cultivating life and beauty. I never heard her say we "had" to water or weed or hoe but only "it's time for us to. . . ." For her, gardening was a privilege and an honor, but she was always careful to explain that gardening came with no guarantee. Just because we labored away in the flower beds didn't necessarily mean that they would bloom as brilliantly or as abundantly as we hoped.

One year, her climbing yellow roses, which were usually covered with magnificent blooms all summer, produced a few buds in the spring and then were barren. I was deeply disappointed and felt that I had done something wrong, since it had been my job to take care of the roses the past fall. A small part of me felt cheated because I had hoped the roses would be even more beautiful than usual and then Mamaw Tribby would compliment me on my green thumb! After I complained about them for the umpteenth time, she sat me down and looked me straight in the eye. "Since when do you know better than God what was to become of these roses? They are perfect just the way they are." I stole a glance at the roses to see if I was missing something. "All we can do in life is our best and then accept what God gives us in return. If God wants us to have roses, we'll have them. If not, all the fertilizer in the world won't do any good."

Lessons from the Gardener's Journal

When the Daffodils Fade

Few things in gardening are as satisfying with so little effort as bulbs. We bury knotty little brown pebbles in the ground in October with an unquestioning belief that they'll be transformed into flowers in April—and they usually are! The biggest problem with bulb gardening is dealing with the ugly yellow foliage after the flowers have gone. In order to have blooms next year, the energy that produced the flower has to flow back down into the bulb, so you'll need to leave the leaves until the stalk breaks off in your hand at the slightest touch. In May and early June when so many early-blooming perennials like irises, peonies, poppies, and roses are glorious, it's depressing to look out on a garden full of dying tulip leaves. For this reason alone, many gardeners—especially those with small areas who have to make every inch count—plant only a few bulbs and miss one of nature's most charming gifts. Over the years I've experimented with a number of ways to make the transition from bulbs to flowers more graceful. Although none of them completely eliminates the mess caused by yellowing foliage, the one piece of advice I can give without reservation is, don't let a spring go by without tulips and daffodils!

I wandered lonely as a cloud
That floats on high o'er vales and hills,
When all at once I saw a crowd,
A host, of golden daffodils;
Beside the lake, beneath the trees,
Fluttering and dancing in the breeze.
　—William Wordsworth,
　　"I Wandered Lonely as a Cloud,"
　　Poems of the Imagination, no. xii

Dealing with Bulb Foliage

1. Treat non-naturalizing bulbs, such as tulips, as annuals. Unless labeled otherwise, tulips are not really perennials and can't be counted on to produce strong repeat blooms.

2. Plant naturalizing bulbs like daffodils in areas where flowering shrubs and other eye-catchers will provide continuous blooms and create a distraction from the yellowing leaves.

3. Grow other compatible plants around bulbs to cover the worst part of the foliage. Daylilies provide a perfect camouflage for yellowing tulips. Pansies, moss pinks, dianthus, and bleeding heart are some of the early-blooming perennials I use to camouflage dying foliage.

4. Cut the stem of daffodils and tie the foliage back by stringing one of the leaves loosely around a cluster of those remaining.

5. Transplant the entire bulb, making sure not to disturb the root system or the foliage, to a secluded spot in a bed or border. This is risky—don't try it unless you are willing to sacrifice the bulb.

When Wordsworth's heart with pleasure filled at a crowd of golden daffodils, it's a safe bet he didn't see them two weeks later.
—Geoff Hamilton

The Magic of Mulching

A birdie with a yellow bill
Hopped upon the window sill,
Cocked his shining eye and said:
"Ain't you 'shamed, you sleepy-head?"
    —Robert Louis Stevenson, "Time to Rise"

One of the first lessons most people learn about gardening is that mulching helps to control weeds and protects against drought. All kinds of natural and man-made materials from old carpet to peanut hulls can be used for mulch. The packaged commercial mulches usually consist of wood bark or chips, which look pretty on flower gardens but are expensive—especially if you are covering a large area. Laying two to three inches of chips in my flower garden and on all the beds and borders can cost several hundred dollars. If you try to skimp on the depth, you may as well not mulch. The weeds pop through as if your paltry layer of mulch was fertilizer. I've read that after you have established a thick base of mulch you will not need to apply as much the next year. It seems I do a lot of mulching every year no matter what. Of course, you can use a layer of black plastic with a thin cosmetic cover of chips over it, but I plant and transplant so frequently that it defeats the purpose of the cover. With organic mulches transplanting is easy. Just move the mulch to one side, put the soil you remove in a pan so you don't mix it with the mulch, then place it around the base of the newly transplanted root ball and replace the mulch. In addition, the man-made mulches don't allow your soil to breathe or give it the benefits of nutrients from decomposing organic matter.

The best solution I've found is to use "homemade" wood chips. There is usually a friend, neighbor, or landscaper eager to unload wood chips made while clearing a lot or felling a tree, and a truckload of these costs a fraction of the price of the commercial ones. Some communities are now making new wood chips available to residents as a means of recycling trees that have fallen. If you do use new wood chips, they should be properly composted for a few months before you apply them. This is easily done by piling them in three-foot squares and stirring and watering them a couple of times a month. I now mulch as much as I need without thinking of the cost—and it's much easier. I simply shovel it into a wheelbarrow and pour it into place. Just about every gardener I know dreads lugging those bulky, heavy plastic bags of mulch and the backache that follows. By using recycled chips, you're keeping trees and shrubs out of landfills and saving yourself hours of weeding.

> I am God in nature; I am a weed by the wall.
> —Ralph Waldo Emerson, "Circles"

Sluggin' It Out

> We have descended into the garden and caught 300 slugs. How I love the mixture of the beautiful and the squalid in gardening. It makes it so lifelike.
>
> —Evelyn Underhill

Like many gardeners, my first encounter with slugs was reminiscent of a scene from an old-fashioned science fiction movie. For days I was mystified by the huge holes that were appearing in the leaves of everything in the garden. I was horrified—soon nothing would be left except spiny skeletons of the precious flowers I had so lovingly set out just a few weeks before. Then one night I happened to look at my delphiniums as I was coming in from the garage. Yuck! Disgusting gray blobs were dangling all over them. These primitive creatures that looked like

they had escaped from a test tube were systematically devouring everything in sight. I felt totally helpless and repulsed at the same time, but by the next morning I was ready to plan my attack. I first sought help at the local garden center, where they didn't blink an eye—I wasn't the only one with this problem. We'd been having a particularly damp and cool spring so these ugly beasts had just about taken over everybody's garden. This news left me feeling better—at least this scourge wasn't personal.

Since then I've learned that slug control must start early before they get the upper hand and do too much damage. Like many of the less pleasant aspects of life, you can't just ignore them and hope they will go away. They just get bigger and bigger—thanks to their diet of tender green leaves from your flower beds. Some plants seem to have a natural immunity to slugs while others are the first to be devoured. If you find slugs are a serious problem, a natural, painless way to minimize their damage is to rely upon plants they find repellent. These include balloon flowers, bleeding heart, coralbells, coreopsis, Jacob's ladder, and hairy flowers—like tuberous begonias and poppies.

Unfortunately, slugs and I share some favorites like dahlias and delphiniums. Vulnerable plants like these get early and frequent applications of slug pellets, which take care of the problem until the weather dries.

If you prefer a natural approach, there are a number of remedies from the kitchen that involve trapping techniques. They require a little more contact with nature's underbelly than I'm looking for, so I reach for the slug pellets. A word of caution, though. Even if you use pellets, you may come across a stray slug when you least expect it. I keep a jar of salt water handy to drop wayward slugs into, along with a jar of gasoline for Japanese beetles. If you are more adventurous than me, here are three techniques that can replace pellets.

Natural Remedies to Combat Slugs

1. *Beer Traps*

Probably the most frequently used natural remedy is a beer trap. At the base of the flower dig a hole large enough for a small tuna fish can, leaving the rim one to two inches above ground level (this will prevent helpful worms and insects from falling into the trap). Fill the can with enough beer to cover the bottom.

2. *Grapefruit Rinds*

The easiest method is to place grapefruit rinds in the garden with the pulp side facing up. The slugs cluster there and can be thrown away with the rind. However, the rinds need to be replaced frequently. If you have a large garden, you'll need a steady supply of grapefruit rinds.

3. *Salt*

Salt can also be used as a weapon since it kills slugs immediately. Since slugs are night feeders, relying on salt baths as your primary method of control means you have to go on nighttime safaris as often as several times a week in damp weather.

Then seek your job with thankfulness and work till further orders,
If it's only netting strawberries or killing slugs on borders;
And when your back stops aching and your hands begin to harden,
You will find yourself a partner in the Glory of the Garden.
　　　　　—Rudyard Kipling, "The Glory of the Garden"

Frittata of Spring Herbs and Wild Mushrooms

I learned from Daddy to garden very early in the morning, shortly after sunrise. He claims it's to take advantage of the coolest part of the day, but I've always suspected other reasons harder to explain. Who could resist seeing sunrise sprinkle golden light over the garden and give birth to a new day? I wonder what more heaven could offer as I putter and poke. After a few hours of laboring in the sunshine, I'm just another hungry, sweaty gardener looking forward to a hearty breakfast. This frittata is the perfect answer.

Heat a third of a cup of extra-virgin olive oil in a cast-iron skillet. Sauté a finely chopped garlic clove, a small Vidalia onion, chopped, and one cup of chopped mushrooms in the oil for about five minutes or until the vegetables are soft. Use a whisk to beat six large eggs with two tablespoons of water and three tablespoons of fresh, finely chopped dill until mixed. Spread the vegetables evenly in the bottom of the skillet and pour the egg mixture over them. Add salt and freshly ground black pepper to taste. Cook until the eggs begin to get firm—just a few minutes. Remove from the flame and sprinkle a third of a cup of freshly grated pecorino Romano cheese on top. Place in a 450-degree oven until the cheese bubbles and the egg is cooked. Slice in wedges and serve with large chunks of toasted homemade rustic bread, orange marmalade, and strong coffee. Serves three.

If, after exercise, we feed sparingly, the digestion will be easy and good, the body lightsome, the temper cheerful, and all the animal functions performed agreeably.
—Benjamin Franklin,
"The Art of Procuring
Pleasant Dreams"

A Eucalyptus and Camphor Milk Bath

Perspiration should flow only after toil.
—Seneca

After a long day in the garden when every muscle in my body is screaming for attention, I take a eucalyptus and camphor milk bath. As the tub is filling, add the following ingredients in this order, swirling each: a twelve-ounce can of evaporated milk, eight to ten drops of eucalyptus oil and eight to ten drops of camphor oil. The water should be hot to the touch. Both eucalyptus and camphor are well-known herbal treatments for arthritis pain. The milk absorbs the oils and coats the skin, prolonging the treatment. If the water is too hot to be comfortable, sit on the edge of the tub and soak your feet; then, when you've adjusted to the temperature, sink into the tub completely. Breathe deeply; the eucalyptus will open your chest, cleanse your pores, and soothe your muscles. Soak for twenty minutes. This is heaven!

3

Simple Dreams

Shade Garden

Patio

Roses
Iris

Garden Shed

Hostas

Vegetables

Iris

Plum

Compost

Rose Garden

Flowering Shrubs

Perennial Bed

"The sun is shining—the sun is shining. That is the Magic. The flowers are growing—the roots are stirring. That is the Magic. Being alive is the Magic—being strong is the Magic. The Magic is in me—the Magic is in me. It is in me—it is in me. It's in every one of us. . . ."
—Colin's chant from *The Secret Garden*,
Frances Hodgson Burnett

A spirited hodgepodge of shrubs, evergreens, and flowers surrounds my house. It's an informal work in progress and so much a reflection of me, it could be a self-portrait. Although I've always loved our yard, I shied away from the commitment required to make it meet all my expectations. Too often I planted around clogged beds and borders instead of ripping them out and starting all over. Last winter as I immersed myself in gardening books and nursery catalogs, my dreams exploded into an elaborate wish list. I wanted a separate area to devote to old English roses and new tea roses. A tiny patch for lettuce, tomatoes, and herbs was on my list, along with more space for lilies and a shade garden for astilbes, ferns, and hostas. The size of our yard is large for a village Colonial but small for a gardener with endless dreams.

By early March I began to talk about moving to a house with more land where we could start over and make a perfect garden. Michael thought I was crazy but was good-natured enough to let me drag him house hunting for a day. After tramping through several places with "fatal flaws"—like the major highway a hundred feet from the front door—I knew he was right. We needed to stay right where we were. I looked at my perennial bed and told myself, "Be happy with what you have."

Then April came and my gardening was in full swing. I dove into the tangle of raspberries in front of the garden shed and started pulling them up without a real plan in mind. As I kept tugging, an idea for a little kitchen garden began to form. In just a few hours, the raspberries were gone. I'd turned and composted the ground and edged my plot with old bricks that had been stacked beside the garage. I ran out to a couple of nurseries where I found five different kinds of lettuce, and returned to plant them all along with dill, tarragon, and arugula seeds with space left over for tomatoes and more herbs.

Few things in life have given me as much satisfaction as replacing the overgrown raspberries with my first true vegetable garden. As I admired my accomplishment, I started looking around the entire lot through new eyes. A large area under a tree where grass refused to grow was almost begging me to turn it into a shade garden. I filled it with divisions from the astile and lilyturf in the backyard and transplanted daylilies and Japanese irises from a border in the front yard. I hoped that the few hours of early-morning and late-afternoon sun would be enough for the more sun-loving lilies and irises. For years I wanted yellow floribunda roses in the front border but I didn't know what to do with those masses of thriving daylilies and irises. As soon as they were in their new home, five yellow "Mirabella" roses moved in to cheer up the front border.

Michael asked if there were other areas I should tackle while I was at it. We both agreed the next project would be my perennial bed with its retaining wall of stacked brick that collapses every few months. He carefully inspected the area and pronounced that we didn't need a retaining wall at all—the slope could be filled in with soil. While I was removing the bricks, I looked at the large expanse of lawn to the left of the perennial bed—a yummy spot with several hours of sun. The words "rose garden" came out of nowhere. Sure enough, within two weeks, I marked off the space, removed the sod, and discovered rich, dark soil underneath. That afternoon I made a lovely brick edging from the former retaining wall and my rose garden was born. As I looked around, I realized my wish list had come to life. With the exception of the roses, my dreams had been here all along, just waiting for me to make them come true.

All things seem possible in May.
  —Edwin Way Teale, "North with the Spring"

Wisdom from
Mamaw Tribby's Garden

There is simply the rose; it is perfect in every moment of its
existence.

—Ralph Waldo Emerson

As a child, I learned that change is a constant companion in
the garden. In my heart I understand that change is nature's gift,
a way of taking us—sometimes gently by the hand and, if that
doesn't work, with a cosmic kick in the seat—toward new experi-
ences so we will reach for tomorrow. Mamaw Tribby used to point
out the changes—large and small—that took place every day.
Sometimes they were almost imperceptible: buds were always
forming, blooms were either beginning to peak or approaching
their decline. Other times, like after the first frost, the entire garden looked transformed overnight. She said, "Just because something changes doesn't mean it's better or worse than the way it
used to be. The old way just doesn't fit anymore. It's time to find
a new way. How can a rosebud be compared to an open blossom?
Is one more beautiful than the other? Is the rosebud less of a rose
because its petals are closed? When the flower is completely open

just before the petals drop, is this the perfect rose? Whether it's a bud, an open blossom, or a dried bouquet, each rose is still a rose."

As I hear Mamaw Tribby talking about the stages of a rose's life I know that despite the successes and failures I've experienced, my inner self has always been the same, and the passing of time will never alter it.

> Because the rose must fade,
> Shall I not love the rose?
> —Richard Watts Gilder, "Song"

Lessons from the Gardener's Journal

The Joy of Painting with Flowers

In his garden every man may be his own artist without apology or explanation.

—Louise Beebe Wilder, *Color in My Garden*

Finding new and exciting ways to use color is one of the most satisfying aspects of gardening. I watched my first husband, who was a painter, look at a canvas, step back and think, then dab on another blob of paint. He would try a splash of burnt sienna next to cobalt blue to see if he liked the effect. He said an inner voice guided him. "Try this," it said. Then, "Oops! Do it over again with this color." I often think of him when I'm redesigning my beds for spring.

Long before it's time to actually make purchases I review the garden photos from the past summer. Every year I take several rolls of film of the entire garden each month from April through September. I'm not as rigorous the rest of the year, but I usually keep some visual record. Notes are great to remind me of what I did and what worked, but they just don't capture the overall effect like photos. When the perennials begin to spring up, I mark the color of what is currently in the garden on typing paper using Magic Markers in many shades of blue, pink, and yellow to pick up the subtle differences. For example, violet blue German bearded irises, purple Japanese irises, and salvia can't all be represented by the same colored marker. I do the same thing for each month—reflecting the blooming times of different flowers. With a thin black ballpoint I circle big empty spaces on each page. These represent areas that require new planting. Then I ask myself a lot of questions: What patterns emerge? Is there a ribbon of one color flowing through the garden? Is there an overall effect or is it hopelessly jumbled? Do I have intense colors competing with each other? What's happening next to the orange flowers like Oriental poppies, daylilies, tree azaleas, that I find the most difficult to work with? Do the blues have yellows or white nearby to make them more visible? Have I used the reds like exclamation points—sparingly but to focus attention? It isn't scientific, but it's easy and helps a nonartist like myself to concentrate on color.

In looking through my monthly photos and hand-drawn journals, I've learned that the shape and size of the plant, as well as the texture and color of its foliage, will influence how well things work together. Although the roses in my garden are many different colors, the effect is softened because they have a similar shape and foliage. Location is a factor as well. The front of the house is busy with windows and columns, as well as the brick walk, patio, and container plants. Most of the borders are made up of a single flower—irises under the dining-room window, daylilies to the left of the walk, peonies to the right, yellow roses in front of the hedge, and rhododendrons in front of the porch—to reduce distractions. Careful scrutiny of garden photos in magazines and books and visiting public gardens before planting helped me to visualize what would work best in these areas.

Flowers have an expression of countenance as much as men or animals. Some seem to smile; some have a sad expression; some are pensive and diffident; others again are plain, honest and upright, like the broad-faced sunflower and the hollyhock.
>   —Henry Ward Beecher,
>   "Star Papers: A Discourse of Flowers"

Four Basic Rules for Using Color

1. Repeat the same color or flower in different areas to unify an entire bed. I've often used rudbeckia this way.

2. Use neutrals to soften the transition from one bright color to another. White and foliage plants, like hostas or artemisias, were almost exclusively used in the past, but purple is growing in popularity as a neutral.

3. The classic combinations are those that pair opposites on the color wheel—the complementary colors. These are: yellow and violet, blue and orange, and red and green. The perfection of yellow and violet is never shown off better than in pansies.

4. An effective way to create harmony is to use plants that are different shades of the same color.

I myself am quite absorbed by the immeasurable plain with cornfields against the hills, immense as a delicate yellow, delicate soft green, delicate violet of a ploughed and weeded piece of soil, regularly chequered by the green of flowering potato-plants, everything under a sky with delicate blue, white, pink, violet tones.
—Vincent van Gogh, letter from Auvers-sur-Oise, France, to his mother and sister, 1890

Painting in the Shade

All these plants demand a degree of shade, but not too much. They spread their leaves and open their flowers before the leaves have fully opened on the trees above them, then settle back gratefully to a Summer of shade.
—Hal Borland,
Beyond Your Doorstep: A Handbook to the Country

Shade is a challenge to new gardeners. While a completely shaded garden does mean you aren't likely to grow roses, I've found that plants that do well in full sun are often fine in partial shade and partial shade lovers can be equally happy in full shade. Even some species of sunflowers do well in the shade. My childhood favorite that Daddy still grows, the giant Maximilian sunflower, will tolerate partial shade. Like any painting, gardens look their best when there is a play of light and shadow. One of my favorite parts of our garden is a shady border planted with the elegant tall yellow spikes of ligularia, white old gooseneck, and Siberian catmint around flowering dogwood and rhododendron. I've learned that shade doesn't have to be a hindrance to your creativity—it just takes a more subtle turn.

Astilbe	Lily-of-the-valley
Bee balm	Lobelia (vedrariensis)
Begonia	Lysimachia
Bleeding heart	Nicotiana
Columbine	Pansies
Early bulbs	Phlox (ozarkana)
Ferns	Primrose
Hosta	Prunella
Hydrangea	Siberian catmint
Ligularia (if damp)	Sunflower (helianthus, Maximilian)

Rice in Rosewater and Turkish Meatballs

> And the rose herself has got
> Perfume which on earth is not.
> —John Keats, "Bards of Passion and of Mirth"

This almost foolproof dish appeals to all of the senses! The subtle fragrance of rice cooked in rosewater is decidedly exotic. Served on a large platter, it makes a wonderful, dramatic presentation. It's delicious and the nuts give it a crunchy texture. Little wonder it's long been one of my favorites for entertaining.

Bring two and three-quarters cups of fresh cold water and one cup of rosewater to a boil. Add two cups of washed basmati rice and return to a boil, then turn the flame down to low and cover. Cook for fifteen to twenty minutes without removing the lid until the rice has tiny holes in the top and all the water has been absorbed. I find with basmati its aromatic smell tells you when it's done. Keep covered to stay warm. Pour a half cup of extra-virgin olive oil into the bottom of a cast-iron skillet. Heat over a low flame. Add four ounces of slivered almonds and brown for a minute. Add one cup of raisins. Stir constantly to keep from burning until the raisins plump up. Cook a few seconds longer. The almonds should be browned. Spread the rice evenly on a platter and pour the raisin-and-nut mixture over the rice and serve with Turkish meatballs circled around the edge of the platter.

To make the meatballs, combine two pounds of ground lamb, half a loaf of whole-wheat pita bread broken into tiny pieces and soaked in a quarter cup of milk, and one slightly beaten egg. Add one teaspoon of garlic powder, one teaspoon of salt, one teaspoon of cinnamon, pepper to taste, and a half cup of drained capers. Mix well and make meatballs about two inches in diameter. Fry until brown on all sides. Makes eight to ten meatballs.

"Intoxicating" Rosewater

When the first roses have fully opened in late spring I select some fresh petals to make my own rosewater. If you normally spray your roses, make sure you leave a bush untreated to use for cooking. Gently wash the rose petals in a large colander. Using an enamel saucepan, cover them with cold filtered water and simmer over a low flame until it comes to a boil Let cool and strain into bottles. The rosewater will keep several weeks refrigerated or longer frozen in ice cubes. Red roses make the prettiest rosewater—a delicate pink color. White, apricot, and yellow roses turn the water an ugly brown, although the intoxicating aroma is the same.

I'd rather have roses on the table
than diamonds on my neck.
  —Emma Goldman

Summer

The Flowering

The leaf becomes flower when it loves.
The flower becomes fruit when it worships.
—Rabindranath Tagore, *Stray Birds*

4

The Garden's Heart

Here with me she used to play,
Here she served pretending tea.
Here on many a yesterday
She walked the garden round with me.
This the bush we planted small,
This the tree that held her swing.
Strange how many memories fall
Round the commonest things.
        —Mamaw Tribby, 1951

If love were what the rose is,
And I were like the leaf,
Our lives would grow together
In sad or singing weather.
                —Swinburne, "A Match"

I think of the patio as the heart of our garden because it holds so many memories. It's a private place where Michael and I have shared our happiest moments. Passing time there evokes the sense of belonging and security that comes from putting down roots. For me it's not surprising—I'm surrounded by my garden. But Michael, who isn't a gardener, is also strengthened and nurtured here. As soon as the weather warms up we move to the patio. It becomes an all-purpose dining and family room as well as coffee nook. During the week we carve out an extra fifteen minutes in the early-morning quiet to have coffee there before I drive him to the commuter train. From the middle of May through September, it's as close as we get to paradise. Over the last few years we haven't been able to bring ourselves to take a summer vacation and leave the patio. Where would we find more pleasure than this? we reasoned.

When we added the patio to the house five years ago, Michael did a lot of thinking about how to make it fit the house's Federal style. He finally decided that it needed a classical railing. To our amazement we found perfect fat, historically accurate balusters at a garage sale! Unfortunately they were covered with many layers of yucky dark varnish. We stripped all thirty-two of them on the hottest weekend of the summer—telling each other that the more work we put into the railing the more we would appreciate the result.

After we finished Michael's beautiful railing, the outdoor furniture looked dilapidated by comparison. For years we had been trying to find the perfect patio set, but the choices were discouraging. The new wood and metal styles were either too large-scale for our house, uncomfortable, expensive, or all three! Though not romantic by most people's standards, we finally decided to get patio furniture for our tenth wedding anniversary. We began the glorious summer day with a visit to a local furniture store but still had no luck. Our spirits were only slightly dimmed as we drove on to Ulster County—home for most of our married life. Beloved mountain country roads greeted us like old friends. Eventually we reached our destination, the restaurant where we were married—The Depuy Canal House, in High Falls, New York. John Novi, its gifted chef and founder, made us a replica of our wedding cake and let us spend the night in his sister's secluded mountain cabin. We felt like newlyweds. The feeling continued the next day as we were inspired by the elegant old gardens of Montgomery Place, Olana, and Clermont—magnificent Hudson River estates now open to the public.

On the way home after a long, memorable day we approached Hyde Park, just before 5:00 P.M. I told Michael we should try to get to the antique center before it closed because it just might have the patio furniture we were looking for. He laughed, because for the past three years I'd been saying this every time I wanted to stop at an antique store. The owners were closing shop so we hurried through the many rooms. Then, at the same time, we saw it, tucked away in a tiny room in the back. An utterly charming white 1930s iron table with six chairs! Of course, they needed repainting and reupholstering, but they were exactly what we'd been looking for and were the perfect gift to celebrate our ten years of married life.

Other patios may be larger or more elegant, but to me, none is more beautiful. This is the place we created together. We've given it our time, labor, and love—and transformed it from a little wooden porch into our personal sanctuary.

> In green old gardens, hidden away
> From sight of revel and sound of strife, . . .
> Here may I live what life I please,
> Married and buried out of sight.
> —Violet Fane, "In Green Old Gardens"

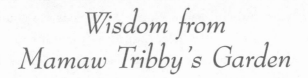

Wisdom from
Mamaw Tribby's Garden

Walk lightly in this garden:
The wind may whisper
    of yesterdays that time
    stilled, not broken.
And, breathe again words heard
    but unspoken.
        —Mamaw Tribby, 1951

On our farm Daddy and my brothers worked in the fields and Mother, my sister, Sue, and I worked in the house. The garden was the only place I ever saw Mother and Daddy working together. I remember as a little girl thinking how nice it was to see the two of them side by side helping each other set out tomato stakes or pick strawberries. I once asked Mamaw Tribby why they didn't work together more often and she threw her head back and laughed so hard I thought she would cry. She said, "Why, this way they can argue about who works the hardest one day and give each other sympathy the next."

Before Mother left home, Mamaw Tribby taught her how important it is for a husband and wife to share the gardening. "All marriages have their hard times," she said with a knowing look, "and when that happens a couple can get closer in the garden than anywhere. The potatoes have to be hoed regardless of what else is going on. You just naturally find yourself saying the things that might be hard to talk about but need to be said anyway. The best talks always take place in the garden."

Lessons from the Gardener's Journal

Creating a Patio Paradise

> Come on in my tropical garden
> Come on in and have a laugh in
> Taste my sugar cake and my pine drink
> Come on in please come on in
>   —Grace Nichols, "Come On into My Tropical Garden"

My favorite way to "dress" the patio for summer is to replicate a tropical garden overflowing with the vibrant oranges, yellows, purples, and
reds of bougainvillea, hibiscus, allamanda, and mandevilla. These exotic flowers I've come to love during vacations in Florida and the
Caribbean thrive in our hot East Coast summers. During the winter I
keep the plants alive by bringing them into the house. Then, in early
June when I move them back to the patio, they are ready to burst into
bloom. Many of my favorites were started several years ago in tiny
three-inch pots. After an afternoon of weeding and watering, there is
no greater reward than stretching out on the patio in a favorite chair
surrounded by giant pots of luxuriant, intoxicating, tropical flowers.

The endless possibilities of container gardening were opened up to
me when I discovered Sun Valley, a local nursery specializing in finished planters and the most perfect bedding and container plants I've
seen anywhere. The owners of Sun Valley create breathtaking designs
with an extraordinary array of blooming flowers. Magnificent tiered
arrangements in antique pots burst with harmonious combinations of
bulbs, perennials, roses, tropicals, and annuals. The tropicals—especially a four-foot hibiscus trained into a tree or a standard covered with
orange or yellow trumpets surrounded by flowing tendrils of lantana,
verbena, and white jasmine—bring images of an island paradise. I've
tried to duplicate these masterpieces with varying degrees of success,
but containers with the standard hibiscus or standard rose are among
those most difficult to maintain. The key to success is keeping the

standard plant in a separate pot set inside a larger one filled with additional flowers. The use of two containers ensures that the plants don't compete with each other for nutrients and water.

Among the most common mistakes typically made with container plantings are not providing the right light for the plants, lack of drainage, and overwatering. In addition, using the right mix for the soil is critical. In an effort to save money or avoid a trip to the nursery, I've filled containers with garden soil only to discover it turns into a rocklike clump. I've also been equally disappointed in the soilless commercial mixes, which do not retain moisture. I make my own soil using a bag of commercial mix as a base and adding two coffee can–fuls of composted manure and a couple of shovelfuls of good garden soil and stirring well.

Suggestions for Spectacular Patio Pots

❧ Group plants by light requirements such as shade, half-sun, and full-sun containers, making certain that all of the plants in one pot have the same preference for a damp or dry environment.

❧ Start with larger specimens rather than small plugs, which take longer to grow into the abundant lush look that is most desirable.

❧ Consider the pot or container in selecting the plants. Make sure the pot is large enough to accommodate the root growth of all the plants over the next six months. A very large pot needs at least one tall center plant with slightly shorter plants surrounding it. Of course, the entire pot could consist of tall plants, or a small trellis with a vine such as a mandevilla. Although concrete and terra-cotta are beautiful, they do absorb water and become so heavy when filled that mobility is virtually impossible. If you do choose to use terra-cotta pots, they should be soaked for twenty-four hours before using—otherwise they steal water from the plants. Some new lightweight fiberglass and plastic planters that simulate natural materials are so practical they are worth trying.

❧ Good drainage is essential and can be achieved by ensuring that the pot has holes in the bottom and adding a layer of gravel or pieces of broken terra-cotta pots.

❧ Use a good potting soil made up of peat moss, sand, compost, and topsoil. Commercial mixes are fine as long as they contain soil.

❧ Apply a 20-20-20 fertilizer every other week. Plants in containers are totally dependent on what you feed them for nourishment, and a lushly planted container is filled with competitors for nutrition.

Water according to the weather and soil. Plants in the hot summer sun will probably need to be watered once a day, but in cooler weather, every two or three days may be sufficient. Some plants, like geraniums, begonias, impatiens, and tropical plants, prefer getting dry before watering, while others like a continuously damp environment.

TROPICAL PLANTS TO COMBINE FOR A FULL-SUN CONTAINER

Bougainvillea	Lantana
Hibiscus	Jasmine
Allamanda	Solanum
Mandevilla	
Silene pendula	

PLANTS TO COMBINE FOR A PART-SUN CONTAINER

Scented and ivy geraniums	Lobelia
Heliotrope	Nierembergia
Verbena	Nicotiana
New Guinea impatiens	Lisianthus

PLANTS TO COMBINE FOR A SHADE CONTAINER

Hydrangea (macrophylla Pia)   Tuberous begonia

Impatiens   Fuchsia, including single-stemmed varieties

Hypoestes   Sweet peas ("Little Sweetheart")

Marguerite daisy

Long-Blooming Perennials

Certainly one of the joys of this time of year is the excitement of see-ing the first shoots of a beloved plant spring to life. The perennial gar-dener is constantly watching the comings and goings of the garden's long-term inhabitants. The lore of perennial gardening is that you give up the continuous blooming of annuals in exchange for the greater subtlety of perennial color and a return engagement next year. However, many things determine whether or not the perennial will sur-vive from year to year. One common cause of plant loss is early frost. Encouraging autumn dormancy by discontinuing feeding in late sum-mer and watering in the autumn allows the foliage to die and is the best way to protect your plants. With the erratic winters we have had in the Northeast in recent years an even more serious threat is repeat freezing and thawing. During warm periods the plant may come out of dormancy only to be vulnerable to a drop in the temperature. The best way to prevent damage is by mulching with dead leaves or other organ-ic material after the ground has frozen, since the mulch insulates the plant from fluctuations in temperature.

Perennials, like all forms of life, have an expected life span. Some—like peonies—have very long lives, but others—lupines, for example—are short-lived. If a plant hasn't returned, it may have nothing to do with your treatment of it or the weather. It may simply have died of old age.

The good news is that many perennials will give almost as much bloom as annuals. If I rigorously deadhead spent blooms before the flower has gone to seed, the result is amazing. Like most species, perennials have the natural instinct to reproduce. In order to do this they must make seeds. If you intervene and remove flowers before they make seeds, the plant will make more flowers and continue the effort. Some flowers, like most phlox, scabiosa, heliopsis, balloon flowers, bellflowers, and blanket flowers, will extend their blooming period dramatically with careful deadheading. Others, like dianthus, feverfew, and gooseneck, will rebloom. Best of all, these beauties ensure continuous color even when the garden is going through its awkward transitions. Nothing can substitute for knowing the specific requirements for each plant. Some perform better when the foliage is completely cut back or cut back halfway, while others require the removal of spent blooms. With care these perennials will fill your garden with flowers for much of the summer.

Long-Blooming Perennial Selections

Balloon flower: Cut each spent bloom and it just keeps going all summer. The delicate blue is glorious.

Centaurea montana: The perennial cornflower. Lacy blue blooms on long stems from June through August. Cut stems after blooms die.

Coreopsis "Golden Showers": A puffy cloud of yellow graces the garden from June until October. Cut back to half after first blooming.

Cosmos "astrosanguineus": The velvety reddish brown perennial. Blooms all summer long, but store over the winter as a tuber. Remove spent blooms.

Dianthus: So many species—including the classic pinks, sweet william, and pheasant eye—giving charming flashes of every shade of pink. Cut it back after the first blooming and it repeats all summer.

Hollyhocks: Majestic. Both the old-fashioned single blooms and new doubles last all summer. A favorite in Colonial gardens. Remove spent flowers.

Malva: Related to the hollyhock, but smaller, softer blooms. After blooming leave a few flowers to reseed.

Phlox "Rosalinde": Dramatic and vigorous tall pink presence all summer. Remove spent flowers.

Rudbeckia: One of Mamaw Tribby's favorites. Blooms from July 4 until frost.

Scabiosa: The pincushion flower. Give it a little lime and it gives you large blooms for cutting May through November. Remove spent flowers.

Siberian catmint: Long blue spikes that bloom month after month. Trim by half after first blooming.

A plant is like a self-willed man, out of whom we can obtain all which we desire, if we will only treat him his own way.

—Goethe, *Elective Affinities*

Bouquet Gathering

If you would like to brighten my hours,
Just bring me a bunch of yellow flowers.

All I need to erase my gloom,
Is the fragrance of flowers with a yellow bloom.
—Mamaw Tribby, January 1957

Gardeners seem to fall into three categories with regard to cutting the flowers they grow. The largest category—I call them "leavers"—consists of those who cut very little, if at all, from their gardens. I first observed leavers at home. Daddy grows gorgeous zinnias, cosmos, snapdragons, and sunflowers in the garden, but never cuts them. I'll confess to having the stereotyped notion that as a man he's less likely to make bouquets. Then I remember that Mother was a leaver, as is my stepmother, Ruby. As a friend of mine, Holly, who is another leaver, explains: "People like me enjoy flowers much more outside where they belong. Cutting is one less thing to do when I'm swamped with jobs that have to be done. So, why do it?" I fall into the second category— the "hiders"—those who love cut flowers but agonize over every one we take. I search for hidden blooms or fragile stems likely to be damaged in an upcoming rainfall. I can't imagine not filling the house with cut flowers, but I evaluate every stem to ensure I'm not lessening the impact of the garden. The last category consists of "cutters," a few people who grow flowers primarily to make bouquets. Although I don't know anyone who does this, I suspect that deep down I'm a "cutter" at heart.

Whether you cut sparingly or with abandon, there are few greater joys than seeing your home graced with flowers grown with your own love and care.

The Man of the Place brought me a bouquet of wild flowers this morning. . . . I am beginning to learn that it is the sweet, simple things of life which are the real ones after all.

    —Laura Ingalls Wilder, "A Bouquet of Wild Flowers," 1917

Raspberry Bread Pudding

After pulling my raspberry bushes this spring my biggest regret was not having fresh berries to make one of Michael's favorite desserts, raspberry bread pudding. We have to make choices, I told myself, but was happy to discover that this dessert is equally good made with frozen berries.

Using an electric mixer, beat a quarter cup of butter or margarine and a third of a cup of sugar until crumbly. Put three egg yolks in a measuring cup and add enough milk to measure three-quarters cup. If you want to make a low-cholesterol dessert, three-quarters cup of a frozen egg substitute, thawed, can be used instead. Gradually mix the milk and eggs, or egg substitute, into the butter and sugar. Mix in a half teaspoon of almond extract and a quarter cup of orange marmalade—type fruit spread.

Cut or tear a loaf of day-old Italian bread into one-inch squares, making a total of six cups. Use the top crust but don't use the bottom crust. Soak the bread pieces in one and three-quarters cup of milk until all the liquid is absorbed.

Beat three egg whites until stiff but not dry, adding a pinch of salt. Fold the egg yolk mixture into the bread and then fold the egg whites into the egg yolks and bread. Spread about two-thirds of the mixture into the bottom of a buttered nine-by-nine-inch pan.

Add about three-quarters cup of sugar (or to taste) to two cups of fresh or twelve ounces of frozen raspberries and gently mix, being careful not to break the berries. Sprinkle on top of the bread mixture and add the remainder. Slightly mingle the berries with the bread. Bake in a preheated oven at 375 degrees for forty-five minutes or until the exposed pieces of bread have browned nicely. Serve warm, plain, or with whipped cream. Serves six.

> So we grew together, . . .
> Two lovely berries molded on one stem.
> —Shakespeare, *A Midsummer Night's Dream*

Making Long-Lasting Bouquets

🌼 Cut flowers in the morning when the water and sugar content is at its peak. Place each stem separately on a flat basket as you cut. This is essential for flowers with large heads like peonies. Take a jar filled with water outside to put the flowers in as soon as possible.

🌼 Use very sharp scissors to cut at an angle in order to give the flower the largest drinking area possible.

🌼 Strip or crush the foliage from the flower below the waterline to reduce bacteria. There are stem strippers available that even remove the thorns from roses.

🌼 Use a hammer to crush woody stems from flowering shrubs to ensure they can take in water.

🌼 Hold the stems of poppies and hollyhocks over a flame for a few seconds to close off their stems and keep them from losing moisture.

🌼 Remove spent blossoms every day. Some vertical flowers, like snapdragons or gladiolus, will continue blooming up the stem for a couple of weeks.

ᨅ Change the water at least every few days and cut one inch to one and a half inches off the stem. Often the bottom of the stem will discolor. Remove this and cut where the stem is still green.

ᨅ Use a fertilizer especially made for cut flowers.

ᨅ Rearrange bouquets as stems become shorter.

ᨅ Keep interesting bottles and jars of all sizes to use as vases. Scatter them all around the house. Often, a single flower is all it takes to change the feeling of a room.

5

Lessons from the Weed Patch

It's a heavy lugubrious day. Fit for no better pursuit than weeding. The brain curdles and not a leaf moves. The blackamoores however bound and tear about like lunatics. I wish cats could be trained to weed gardens.

—Dora Carrington, letter to Lytton Strachey

Our yard is separated from the neighbors' by a small patch of ground between the driveway and a two-foot-high retaining wall. This wall is concrete and finished in a strange pattern of uneven swirls. It's every bit as ugly as it sounds. When we first moved into our house, this patch was planted in German bearded irises, daylilies, and English ivy. It sounds pretty, but in reality the irises and lilies were overgrown and the ivy was mixed with pachysandra and weeds—it was a complete mess. I tried to ignore it, telling myself that at least it hid the unbearable wall during the summer. Yet, every time I got into the car, there it was—a reminder that I was willing to live with this disaster. Although we made many wonderful changes in the house and garden and in our lives since we moved here, they seemed to pale next to this visible sign of neglect.

Our second summer in the house I transplanted some violets from the flower bed, which I thought might be a solution. I quickly learned that if you can't do something right, don't do it at all. Although the violets were breathtaking in May when they were covered with hundreds of tiny purple gemstones, by the end of that summer they were strangling everything. Despite their charm, they were weeds and had to go. The next spring I couldn't bear to pull them up with their delicate amethyst-like blooms intact, so I waited. How devious nature can be when she is protecting her own! By the time I got to them it was July and the roots were so compact and deep they were impossible to budge.

In the meantime, a vision was forming in my mind. I wanted a flowering shrub like rose of Sharon to provide summer height alternated with Japanese euonymus, a shorter vertical evergreen. English ivy seemed the best way to cover the ground and camouflage the wall year round.

Now I had a direction instead of just a thorn in my side. In early June of the following year I tackled the space, determined that these weeds were not going to get the best of me. I carefully moved the irises just after they bloomed, when they could be transplanted most safely. Although the daylilies were only a month from opening, I moved them anyway. The guilt I felt was alleviated when many bloomed despite their recent upheaval. The violets were especially lovely, and I suspected them of trying to seduce me again, but, by now, I was impervious to their charms. When each little violet came out with a gentle tug, I was filled with ridiculous glee at this accomplishment. At some point I asked myself why I was getting so much pleasure from pulling up violets. Like most gardeners I view weeds as a personal enemy, but my reaction still seemed out of proportion to the circumstances. Then I realized that this patch had come to represent my personal limitations and my will to overcome them. One day those smiling violets were my deep-rooted stubbornness and the next day they became my disorganization. During the summer I carefully pulled each returning violet, determined not to tarnish the perfection of this little spot of earth. Now when I survey the ivy, the rose of Sharon, and the euonymus, I reflect on the progress of my own life and my own inner weed patch.

The best I can find to say of these coarse rampageous violets is that they will thrive anywhere. . . .

—Reginald Farrer

Wisdom from
Mamaw Tribby's Garden

What would become of the garden if the gardener treated all the weeds and slugs and birds and trespassers as he would like to be treated, if he were in their place?
    —T. H. Huxley, *Evolution and Ethics*, 1893

Mamaw Tribby knew a lot about weeds and carried on a running commentary about their affairs as we weeded her flower beds or walked about in the woods. No one disliked weeds any more than she did or worked harder to keep them out of the garden, but she loved to draw parallels between people and weeds. "What's the difference between a weed and a flower?" she asked. "Mallow is in the same family as the hollyhock and malva. A lot of weeds, like dandelions or pokeweed, can be eaten. Some, like plantain, are good home remedies if you know how to use them. Buttercups are as pretty as flowers. Raspberries or blackberries can turn into a horrible mess despite their fruit. What is it that makes a useful plant so despised that people will actually use poison to get rid of it?"

The answer always boiled down to one thing—any plant becomes a weed when it steals nourishment, light, and water from its neighbors. "Weeds are selfish thieves. As they get stronger, weeds turn into bullies who crowd out everybody else. If they were people maybe we could teach them how to get along with others."

Lessons
from the
Gardener's Journal

Know Your Competition!

> The richest soil, if uncultivated, produces the rankest weeds.
> —Plutarch, *Lives:* "Coriolanus"

The second year I had a garden I was ready to do anything to prevent slugs. Damp mulch seemed to contribute to the problem, so I decided not to mulch but instead leave the soil of my little flower bed bare. By July I was spending every weekend trying to keep the sweat out of my eyes while I yanked and tugged at my thriving weed bed. Slugs were easier to deal with than this! The battle was lost that summer, but I was determined not to make the same mistake again. This farmer's daughter had learned a basic fact of agriculture—the ground will not remain bare. Plants grow where there is light, soil, and water, whether they are invited or not.

Every gardener develops their own approach to controlling weeds. I've found that learning more about the specific weeds in my garden has gone a long way toward helping me control them. You wouldn't think of planting flowers without knowing their water, light and, hopefully, soil requirements. Even though the goal is to eliminate rather than propagate, weeds are no different. Although there are hundreds of plants that are technically considered weeds, I estimate that I see about twenty in my garden and lawn during the course of the year.

The first piece of essential information is whether a weed is an annual, biennial, or perennial. Annuals germinate from seeds, produce shoots and flowers, sow seeds, and start their life cycle again. One annual, galinsoga, is also called quickweed because it can go through this cycle several times a year. If it seems like you pull it and it grows right back, that's because it does! In addition to quickweed, the annuals I watch out for include: goosegrass, a flat weed that takes over bare spots in the lawn and eventually kills the grass; spotted spurge, even flatter than goosegrass, which forms a fast-spreading mat and is very invasive in hot weather; and purslane, a prolific succulent related to portulaca, which crowds out weaker plants and can be identified by its yellow flowers in the morning. The single most important step in managing all annual weeds is removing the culprit before it goes to seed and propagates.

Biennials germinate in the first year and produce a ground-hugging rosette. The second year they flower, make seeds, and complete their life cycle. If you remove the rosette during the first year, it will eliminate the weed. One of the most visible biennials is Queen Anne's lace, a lovely wildflower that is invasive in the garden.

Perennials are long-living plants that spread in two ways. Like annuals, they develop seeds that sow new plants, but in addition they have deep systems of roots or rhizomes that send up new shoots. The seeds must be prevented from spreading and the root or rhizome must be completely removed to prevent a return of the pest. For the most part, it's the perennials that require that you get out a shovel and dig out the tough, thick snarls that feel like they go all the way to China. Among the perennials with the most tenacious roots are the dandelion, whose root must be dug up completely or it produces several new shoots to replace the one you picked; and the tall, broad-leafed plantain, which is extremely difficult to remove when the plant matures. On the list of really bad perennial weeds is johnson grass, which is best dealt with by exposing the roots so that they will freeze during the winter.

I think of annuals as a common cold: nip it in the bud before it turns into pneumonia. Biennials are like the flu, more serious than a cold, but with time, you recover. Perennials, however, require major surgery to remove. Fortunately, in areas where the ground is cultivated, like a flower garden, annuals are typically the weeds you battle most often.

Weeds . . . are the little vices that beset plant life, and are to be got rid of the best way we know how.

—*Farmer's Almanac, 1881*

A Stitch in Time . . .

It is not enough for a gardener to love flowers; he must also hate weeds.

—Anonymous

Focusing a lot of effort in the first month of the growing season and addressing problems as soon as they appear are the keys to garden maintenance. I've always thought of weeding as the equivalent of housework in the garden and, like housework, a good, thorough spring cleaning is essential. With all the big cultivating and planting jobs that must be done in the spring, it's easy to look at the few tiny weeds and think, "I'll get to them next week." Unfortunately, next week may be too late. Fast-spreading weeds like lamb's-quarters, spurge, and lady's thumb will be greatly reduced if you catch them early enough. In the meantime, perennial weeds get stronger every day. Weeds are fast growers, faster than delphiniums, asters, astilbe, and many other flowers. In the cool conditions of spring, your tender, young flowers are more vulnerable than at any other time to the aggressive attacks of weeds.

It's also important to respond immediately to unusual conditions. A few years ago I noticed a strange, weird, stringlike vine growing on a coreopsis. I pulled it off and felt my skin crawl, though I didn't bother to find out why. When I went back to the garden several days later this monster was suffocating the entire flower! My weed reference book told me this vine was a parasite called dobber. The only remedy is to cut the plant below where the dobber starts and dispose of it in the trash—never the compost heap. I cut the coreopsis back and haven't seen the dobber since. I shudder to think of what would have happened if I had just removed it a few more times without learning how to deal with it.

Steps to Control Weeds

Plant flowers close together to crowd out weeds.

Plant some tall, fast-growing, large-leafed specimens, which discourage weeds by cutting off their light source.

Mulch, mulch, mulch.

Pull weeds after a rain when the soil is loosened.

Always pull weeds out by the roots.

Never allow weeds to flower and reseed.

When necessary don't hesitate to take aggressive action like cutting the plant foliage.

Start a systematic rotating weeding schedule, to reach every bed over a two-week period.

> Now 'tis the spring, and weeds are shallow-rooted;
> Suffer them now, and they'll o'ergrow the garden. . . .
> —Shakespeare, *2 Henry VI*

Seductive Invaders

One of the challenges of perennial gardening is having the will to contain exuberant spreaders. I'm especially torn by rudbeckia. If I didn't exert some control, my entire bed would be overrun with these charming yellow daisies. As much as I love them and appreciate how they contribute to the garden, enough is enough! I've discovered that many flowers have the potential to become destructive if left unchecked. These flowers qualify as weeds by Mamaw Tribby's definition. They bully their neighbors and steal resources.

Bee balm
Daylilies
English daisy
False dragonhead
Goldenrod
Morning glory

Purple loosestrife
Rudbeckia
Speedwell
Violets
Yarrow

And so it criticized each flower,
This so precious seed;
Until it woke one summer hour,
And found itself a weed.
—Mildred Howells, "The Different Seed"

Redeeming Virtues

Shall I not rejoice also at the abundance of the weeds whose seeds are the granary of the birds?
                                   —Henry David Thoreau, *Walden*

Few weeds are so terrible they have no redeeming qualities. I think it's important to pay respect to those virtues as a way of better appreciating how our own tiny garden's ecosystem fits into the universe. Some common weeds are natives, having grown in one area for centuries, if not millennia, as in the case of horsetail. Many of our most serious weed problems, though, came about when plants introduced for a specific purpose turned out to be so well adapted to local growing conditions that they took over—wiping out other plants. I can remember Daddy coming in at lunchtime in the summer thoroughly discouraged by his ongoing battle with johnson grass, which was supposed to be a pasture crop when it was brought to the United States in the 1800s.

Some of the plants we think of as weeds were very helpful to Native Americans and later to the pioneers who learned how to use them. Based on stories I heard while growing up, the Indiana pioneers savored as delicacies many of the wild plants that we now consider weeds. The tender young leaves of pokeweed, red sorrel, yellow dock, and dandelion were all eaten raw or cooked, and dandelion flowers were dipped in batter and fried. Today, many weeds have found their way into health-food stores, where they are used as herbal remedies for a wide variety of conditions.

Barbara's Sorrel Soup

From May to August the meadows are often ruddy with the sorrel, the red leaves of which point out the graves of the Irish rebels who fell at Tara Hill in the "Ninety-eight."

—Folkard, *Plant-lore, Legends, Lyrics*

Our friends Barbara and Dick Chandler have a beautiful walled garden filled with herbs, roses, and perennials. Dick did the charming illustrations that you see throughout these pages, and Barbara graciously volunteered her sorrel soup recipe, which she serves with homemade bread. In a Dutch oven place a whole chicken breast with bone, skinned, and add six cups of water and one bay leaf. Cover and simmer gently over low heat until the chicken comes off the bone, about an hour and a half. Discard the bone and break the chicken into pieces. Thoroughly wash and coarsely chop a quarter pound each of fresh sorrel, spinach, and parsley. Heat a quarter cup of butter in a skillet, add the vegetables, and simmer over low heat for five minutes.

Add to the chicken. Peel four medium potatoes and slice into quarter-inch-thick pieces and add to the chicken. Add salt and pepper to taste and continue cooking over low heat for twenty-five to thirty minutes or until the potatoes are tender. Serves four.

Friends in Disguise

You cannot forget if you would those golden kisses all over the cheeks of the meadow, queerly called "dandelions."
—Henry Ward Beecher

Hard as it is to believe, many of our most familiar weeds are actually herbs with medicinal properties. The common dandelion has been used as an herbal remedy for centuries. The leaves are a natural diuretic, which can be useful during those times you retain water. My friend, herbalist and author Jason Elias, has taught me to make an infusion by rubbing together one ounce of dried dandelion leaves in a clean cloth, then pouring three cups of boiling water over them. Cover and let steep in a stainless-steel or ceramic pitcher for half an hour. Pour through a strainer and drink. This makes enough for one day. Drink a cup, hot or cold, in the morning, at noon, and in the evening. Store in the refrigerator. Although dandelion leaves are considered a safe herb, this treatment should not be used on a prolonged basis. It's always a good idea to consult your doctor before using any herbal remedy.

Another herbal treatment found in the weed patch is plantain. When one of us was stung by a bee, the first thing Mamaw Tribby would do was look for plantain, extract some of the juice from the stalk, and rub it on the sting. It's an emergency remedy that can also be used for other insect bites. If you develop a rash, or the bite worsens, see a doctor.

6

Glory Days

Now it is summer, and as usual, life fills me with transport and I forget to work. This year I have struggled for a long time, but the beauty of the world has conquered me.

—Leo Tolstoi

The spectacular stars of the perennial world—the irises, peonies, poppies; old roses and early clematis—all vanish by the middle of summer. After saturating the garden with color for almost a month, they disappear as quickly as they bloomed. Each year as I survey the garden, my heart sinks as I see how the torrid midsummer temperatures have taken quite a toll on my lush springtime fantasies. Although the more subtle heat-tolerant perennials are just beginning to bloom, they can't compete with the glamorous flower heads of poppies and peonies. Despite the photos in nursery catalogs, the plants that bloom from July through frost have a preponderance of foliage and less dramatic flowers than the earlier-blooming varieties.

My midseason disappointment is soon forgotten as I immerse myself in the countless little tasks necessary for garden maintenance. The false dragonhead and purple loosestrife seem to be everywhere and are not an attractive addition to the garden—off they go to the compost heap. I trim back the asters and chrysanthemums one last time before letting them bud. With a touch more weeding and pruning, some empty spots emerge to plant a few more late-season perennials. This gives me an excuse for my annual pilgrimage to White Flower Farms in Litchfield, Connecticut, the East Coast mecca for perennial gardeners. I return with more asters, monkshood, and sunflowers than I know what to do with.

The garden responds to this attention almost overnight. Summer flowers are everywhere, providing companionship for a picnic on a steamy midsummer day and firefly-watching at dusk. Shades of pink from dianthus, malva, phlox, purple coneflower, yarrow, lilies, and dahlias cluster in the corners. Bluish lavender from salvia, scabiosa, centaurea montana, and asters float in the center of the bed and crawl up the giant delphiniums. Splashes of yellow from rudbeckia, sunflowers, and coreopsis sparkle here and there.

This is my garden's middle age. Its youthful flamboyance is gone, but these midseason colors and shapes *are* every bit as lovely—just more subtle. If I look in a mirror for a long time I can see that my newly acquired midseason curves and shadows are a softer but equally beautiful version of my younger self.

Youth, large, lusty, loving—youth full of grace, force, fascination,
Do you know that Old Age may come after you with equal grace, force, fascination?
                    —Walt Whitman, "Youth, Day, Old Age and Night"

Wisdom from Mamaw Tribby's Garden

Specific flowers—with their vivid scents and colors—awaken our memories and touch our soul. Yellow roses had a special place in Mamaw Tribby's heart. When she lived with my Aunt Ester, an entire wall of their house was covered with a giant climbing bush. We spent many hours tending them and she told us time and again about her first home. It was built by her grandfather, Elisha Collings, when he moved his family from South Carolina to southern Indiana's hill country in the mid-1800s. The house was surrounded by a split-rail fence that had yellow and red roses cascading over it all summer long.

One warm July evening her first boyfriend picked one of those yellow roses and gave it to her when he declared his love. Mamaw Tribby always said, "Fortunately, his love died faster than the roses. He wasn't my true love—that was your grandfather—but he was my first. Who could know how much a yellow rose would mean to me? One sniff of a yellow rose and all of these memories of home and my youth come flooding back. In my heart I become a teenager."

> Where is the heart that does not keep
> some fond remembrance hidden deep?
> Who has not saved some trifling thing—
> a faded yellow flower or a broken ring?
> —Mamaw Tribby, 1952

Lessons
from the
Gardener's Journal

Water Worries

One of the biggest gardening challenges in midsummer is drought. I'm always shocked to see people recklessly use water as if there was an infinite supply. On the farm the water we used came from an old cistern that went dry a couple of times during the summer, forcing us to buy water by the truckload. As children we were taught the importance of turning off faucets and, generally, using as little water as possible. My own habits of water usage have changed little since then, and I've happily noticed that in the last several years water conservation has become more fashionable.

In periods of drought, like we experienced here in the Northeast last summer, many communities are severely restricting the use of water right at the time when the garden is most in need of it. These long dry spells seem to be occurring more and more often. In anticipation of the worst weather summer can bring, I started growing more drought-resistant flowers like rudbeckia, echinacea, artemisia, salvia, and yarrow and making water conservation a regular part of my spring routine.

A Plan for Water Conservation

🍂 Rely on plants that don't need a lot of water. Good choices are ornamental grasses, herbs, hairy plants—like Oriental poppies—and plants that retain water in their leaves—like sedum "Stonecrop." Plants that thrive in the prairie need little water and, unlike typical southwestern plants, tolerate cold winters.

🍂 Prepare the soil for better water efficiency. Daddy stressed that a good gardener always worked with the soil below the surface, deep down where the roots were growing. Sometimes after a little drizzle the ground will form a crust that makes it look deceptively hard. To understand the garden's water needs, it's important to turn the soil several inches deep. Organic material such as humus, compost, and manure ensures that the soil is well aerated and will retain moisture.

🍂 Cultivate the ground deeply when planting. This will encourage the plant to spread its roots down into the subsoil.

🍂 Mulch with a thick layer of material applied around the base of the plants to retain water and reduce evaporation.

🍂 Don't let water run downhill. If you have sloping borders, make a small trough around each plant to trap the water until it can be absorbed.

🍂 Always water early in the morning when the water level of plants is at its highest, and you can really tell which are in the greatest need. Just like people, plants can droop after a day in the scorching sun even though they are really not suffering from lack of water. Daytime watering can burn plants—especially in intense heat. Evening watering can be unhealthy and encourage the growth of fungus, like blackspot on roses or mildew on asters and phlox.

► Water deeply so that you are replenishing the roots. It's actually better not to water at all if you can't water sufficiently because the poor dehydrated plant will go up to the surface to get water and lose its best defense against drought—deep roots. Last summer I used a large funnel to send water directly to the roots and it worked like magic!

► Water the most valuable and the most vulnerable plants first during periods of water restrictions. Woody shrubs are always at the top of my watering list. Some older specimens are almost irreplaceable. Even well-established flowering shrubs may be shallow-rooted and need regular watering. Next on my watering list comes newly planted shrubs, followed by the roses, my little vegetable patch, the perennials, and the annuals. The grass gets no water. It may look like straw but it'll recuperate.

► Use a soaker hose. These are inexpensive and are an excellent solution for long areas like borders.

> . . . men that's lived as long as me
> Has watched the world enough to learn
> They're not the boss of this concern.
>   —James Whitcomb Riley, "Wet-Weather Talk"

What's Wrong When . . .

A garden is an awful responsibility. You never know what you may be aiding to grow it.
   —Charles Dudley Warner, *My Summer in a Garden*

One of the great frustrations of this time of the year is seeing a beloved flower develop yellow leaves and feeling helpless to stop the decline. Although most gardeners aren't interested in becoming plant doctors, a little knowledge of nutrition is essential to avoid over- or underfeeding. You'll also be better prepared to understand problems when they occur.

The main ingredients in fertilizer are the three basic plant food groups: nitrogen, phosphorus, and potassium. The labels on fertilizer tell what percentage of each ingredient is included. The first number always refers to the percentage of nitrogen, the second to the percentage of phosphorus, and the third to the percentage of potassium. For example, 20-20-20 is a balanced high-powered plant food used for container plants and is usually in a water-soluble form for quick absorption. It contains 20 percent nitrogen, 20 percent phosphorus, and 20 percent potassium or potash. The less potent 5-10-5 formulation is typically recommended for perennials. The high percentage of phosphorus ensures good root growth and flower production—very desired in perennials. Nitrogen stimulates the growth of a plant's green stems and foliage. With perennials more nitrogen leads to excessive foliage at the expense of flowers. Potassium, the third plant food group, gives plants vigor, helps to fight diseases, and reduces the need for water. Secondary elements, like calcium, magnesium, and sulfur, are also important in good nutrition, as are trace elements like iron, copper, boron, and others. Like a daily vitamin, most good fertilizers contain these additional nutrients in appropriate amounts.

A lack of nitrogen is often the culprit when the tips of the oldest leaves of a plant start to turn yellow. The yellowing will proceed to the whole leaf. With a phosphorus deficiency the oldest leaves will turn a purplish tint. When potassium is needed, the older leaves are first affected by a yellowing that moves along the leaf seams.

Organic products, such as dried blood and bonemeal, are readily available in garden centers and can be used to fix these problems. Dried blood contains 15-3-0 and is an easy way to add nitrogen. One of the main bulb foods, bonemeal, is high in phosphorus—4-12-0. It helps strengthen the stems of bulbs to support the weight of daffodils and tulips. Wood ashes are a good natural source of potassium—0-1.5-7. Remember, don't fertilize perennials and shrubs late in the summer when they are getting ready for dormancy.

Caring for Roses

One of the great joys of summer is roses. I'd like to dispel any lingering insecurity some of you might have about special talents needed to grow roses. Before I moved here, I'd been afraid to invest too heavily in roses. I told myself it was because I was a "weekend" gardener, but I think it was really just a fear of failure. Since several roses were already flourishing when we moved in, I had to become a rose gardener very quickly—ready or not! I tried to remember everything I'd learned from Mamaw Tribby, as well as doing some old-fashioned research to keep them alive, and I'm proud to say those early inhabitants have thrived. More important, in the six years we've lived here the rose population has grown to twenty-three.

Like most people with small spaces, I want to get the most out of every inch under cultivation, so I'm partial to repeat bloomers. Yet, my Climbing Crimson Beauty is irresistible with its long blooming period in June when it's completely covered in large double flowers with a sweet-spicy scent. Repeat bloomers are generally less hardly because they don't have as long to go into dormancy before cold weather comes. In addition to careful watering and feeding, here are some of the things I've learned to improve my roses.

It will never rain roses: when we want
To have more roses we must plant more trees.
—George Eliot, *The Spanish Gypsy*, Book III

Tips for Growing Gorgeous Roses

1. Read up carefully on the rose you're buying and make sure it fits your needs. Never buy roses impulsively unless you're willing to take a chance.

2. Buy "#1" quality roses. These have a good root system and at least three strong canes growing from the bud union. The foliage on the rose you're buying isn't very important. Focus on the root system. Without it the rose won't survive the winter.

3. As in buying a house, the best advice is "location, location, location." Roses need lots of sun—at least six hours a day with the bulk in the morning, and a little breeze—but no heavy wind and a good distance from other shrubs or plants that may harbor insects.

4. Don't plant a rose where an old one was planted. No one knows exactly why, but the new one is more likely to fail.

5. Allow newly planted roses to develop roots before you fertilize them. I wait about two months, but some experts recommend up to a year. Fertilizer diverts growth to the foliage and away from the roots. The rose will look healthy but may not survive.

6. Prune in the spring before new growth starts. If any suckers are growing from below the bud union, remove the entire growth.

7. Practice good "rose keeping" by cutting out weak shoots, suckers, diseased leaves, and canes. Carefully dispose of diseased leaves to prevent them from infecting other areas. Never compost them. Deadhead as soon as the petals drop, but leave the last roses of the season. They tell the rose to enter dormancy.

8. After hard frost, protect the bud union by packing the crown with soil or compost. Use a little less than a foot for large roses and six inches for smaller ones. Never use peat, since it retains water. Don't hill up the soil around the roses and expose the roots. If winter temperatures in your area stay below 10 degrees for two weeks or more, protect roses by covering the canes with hay, burlap, or pine branches.

Green Bean and Toasted Almond Salad

Green beans are bushy and take up a lot of space in the garden, but I can't resist them because they remind me of the farm. This salad is a wonderful addition to a summer dinner.

Cut the tips off of two pounds of washed green beans. Steam until barely cooked through. Remove from heat and put in a salad bowl. Mince two medium-sized cloves of fresh garlic and add to the beans.

Toss with two tablespoons of extra-virgin olive oil and then squeeze the juice of a quarter of a medium-sized lemon and toss. Salt and pepper to taste. Sauté a third of a cup of slivered almonds until lightly browned in two tablespoons of olive oil. Pour on top of the beans. Cover and refrigerate for several hours until completely chilled. Try with grilled tuna steaks, garden fresh tomatoes "Provencal," and sourdough bread. To make tomatoes "Provencal," cut out the stem, cut in half, rub the tops with garlic, sprinkle a tablespoon of Italian seasoned bread crumbs with Parmesan cheese, drizzle with a few drops of olive oil on the tops, and broil skin side down until brown, about five minutes.

I came to love my rows, my beans, though so many more than I wanted. They attached me to the earth, and so I got strength like Antaeus. But why should I raise them? Only Heaven knows.

> —Henry David Thoreau, *Walden*

Flowers for Drying

Gill Farms, one of New York State's finest farmer's markets, grows field upon field of flowers—sunflowers, snapdragons, cleome, strawflowers, statice, and coneflowers, to name only a few—to sell in their stands. To my great joy, the public can pick to their heart's content. Although I make several trips every summer, it's a special treat in late August when I'm selecting flowers to dry for the winter. The only "technique" I use is to hang the flowers upside down in the attic, tied in bunches of eight to ten. Every year I try new species and I'm always amazed at the results. Statice, strawflower, and honesty plant are primarily grown for dried arrangements, but delphinium and roses also make excellent dried flowers. I've had great success with rosebuds and partially opened roses, less with fully opened ones. The hydrangea is as beautiful dried as fresh, and I have many plants that provide an abundance of blooms for autumn decorations.

Some of the more unusual flowers for drying are the celosia, asters, baby's breath, butterfly weed, globe thistle, and veronica. The seed pods of rudbeckia and sedum "Autumn Joy" and the hips of many roses add unusual shapes to lasting bouquets. Several annuals with lovely silver foliage are lumped together and called "Dusty Miller." Those most commonly found in nurseries are *Senecio cineraria, Senecio vira-vira,* and *Centaurea cineraria.* All are wonderful in dried arrangements or alone in a ceramic pitcher or on a wreath. Dwarf purple heather makes a stunning accent dried upright in the container; I have a few in my living room that have retained their vibrant color for several months. Sometimes it's an effort to make the time to dry flowers, but I'd sorely miss having a supply to decorate the house during the winter.

Autumn

The Bounty

I'm homesick for the golden hills,
The fragrant autumn air.
The sound of whippoorwills at dusk,
The reddened sumac's flare,
The scent of clover and the spice
    of alfalfa, blue as seas,
Dahlias tossing pretty heads
and nodding in the breeze.
                —Mamaw Tribby, 1954

7

Essential Tasks

The sense that we have brought to birth
Out of the cold and heavy soil,
These blessed fruits and flowers of earth
Is large reward for all our toil.
  —Ruth Pitter, "The Diehards"

Autumn gardening decisions—planting trees and shrubs, reseeding a new lawn, designing the way the garden will look until mid-June when the focus on bulbs gives way to perennials—are among the most important of the year. But, sometimes the biggest decisions are those made by default—like my decision not to box in our fig tree for the winter.

When Michael and I moved into our house we were befuddled by a white wooden box over six feet tall and about three feet square standing in the middle of the backyard. The mystery was solved when we learned that it was a fig tree protected for the winter. Figs are rare this far north. They are difficult to grow and often fail to produce fruit. The Elwyns, the previous owners of the house, had been growing the fig for many years with great success. It might have been because the house is nestled between hills and the river and the area is slightly warmer than other areas of Westchester County, but I believe it was because the Elwyns loved the fig tree and spoke of it as if it were a member of the family. The fig responded by thriving under the most challenging circumstances. I liked the idea of the fig tree, but reassembling the box was a formidable job that I always put off until the last minute.

After our second year in the house we decided to build a patio, and the only place that made sense was where the fig tree was growing. We moved the fig and, amazingly, it survived, though it didn't produce fruit that summer. The following autumn, I was especially busy with work and an overly ambitious bulb-planting program, and time seemed to slip away. The fig tree had outgrown the box and building a new one was a major undertaking. I compromised by wrapping the fig in straw and burlap. After it had survived a move in the same year, I knew this was the ultimate insult, and I felt more than a tinge of guilt. Much to my astonishment, the fig was fine. Encouraged by its resilience, when October rolled around the next year I didn't feel nearly so guilty about using the burlap and hay. Then, one bitterly cold morning I looked at the thermometer and saw it was fifteen below. My first thought was

"Oh, no. I've finally killed the fig tree." Sure enough, the fig didn't make it through the winter. I'll never know if it would have lived through those brutal temperatures in the wooden box, but if I had given it the same careful attention and support as the Elwyns it might have had a chance.

> New feet within my garden go,
> New fingers stir the sod, . . .
>
> New children play upon the green,
> New weary sleep below;
> And still the pensive spring returns,
> And still the punctual snow!
> —Emily Dickinson

Wisdom from
Mamaw Tribby's Garden

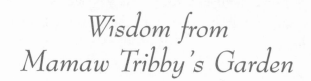

Mamaw Tribby loved gladiolus. Although she intuitively clustered flowers in natural-looking masses, glads were the exception. She called flowers planted in rows "armies" but for some reason known only to her, glads preferred to be planted this way. In her kitchen garden, the rows just behind low-growing vines filled with strawberries, garden peas, and squash were devoted to the precious glads. She carefully planted them over a period of three or four weeks to have a spectacular display of their swordlike stems from the end of July through September. As a child I made bouquets from wildflowers, weeds, any living thing I could find, but I always knew that the glads were off-limits. Mamaw Tribby's glads were there to make the garden pretty.

When the foliage of the early glads began to turn yellow in late September or October, we carefully lifted them out of the ground, shook off the dirt, and let them dry. After a week or two we cut back the foliage and stored them in paper bags. Often my job was to punch ventilation holes in the bag with an ice pick and label the color of the glads on the bag. We continued to do this until all the glads were stored. Sometime around Valentine's Day, Mamaw Tribby would get the bags out of the unheated storeroom where she kept them and we pulled off the little bulblets growing from last year's old corm, which was dried and shriveled. It was hard to believe that glorious three-foot glads in creamy salmons, bright reds, deep pinks, and sunshine yellows had come from those decrepit little rocks. Mamaw Tribby loved to count how many bulblets she got from each corm. The corm and the bulblets went back into the paper bags, ready to be planted in May. This summer the bulblets would only grow foliage, but in a couple of years they would produce full-grown glads. Even as a child it seemed like a lot of trouble to me. One day I asked her why we had to do so much work to have glads. She said, "Caring for something you love isn't work. It's God's way of helping you not to take it for granted."

Lessons from the Gardener's Journal

Special Garden Needs in Autumn

Time and ages, to sow or to gather be bold,
But set to remove, when the weather is cold.
　　　　　　—Thomas Tusser,
　　　　　　　Five Hundred Points of Good Husbandry, 1577

These autumn days—when I'm hurriedly trying to finish the important jobs that must be done this time of year—are among the most
pleasurable in the garden. Despite the sense that winter is in the wind,
I find peace working outside on days warmed by the mellowing sun.
The weather—so perfect for planting—is also perfect for the strenu-
ous labor required to get the garden ready for the hard winters we can
have in the Hudson Valley. By now the muscles in my poor body have
acclimated to gardening and I effortlessly bend, stoop, and lift for several hours without worrying about whether I can get out of bed the
next morning. The leaves of the early-shedding trees are scattered on
the lawn, and walnuts from the tree on the other side of the hedge are
dropping from the sky like hand grenades. The flower garden has
turned into a tangle of asters and dahlias. The Russian sage is suffocating in the shadow of malva, and the cosmos and sunflowers have
grown to the size of small trees. Bringing order to this chaos seems so
overwhelming I can't help but ask myself what would happen if I let it
all go until the spring. That's when I know it's time to make a list—a
sure way to give myself the illusion that I'm in control. I find just looking at it strangely comforting. It reassures me that I have reason to be
overwhelmed and subtly reminds me that putting off these jobs means
I'll have to work twice as hard next spring! Here's the list I've developed over the years.

Autumn "To Do" List

Reaping the Rewards

❧ Cut and dry remaining flowers, such as the last of the hydrangeas or ornamental grasses, which can be used in floral arrangements.

❧ Harvest the last of the herbs, wash them, dry and store them for cooking, potpourri, and teas.

❧ Collect pine cones, bittersweet, leaves, and other natural material for holiday decorations.

❧ Prepare the patio plants and pot the less hearty garden plants to overwinter inside the house and in the basement.

❧ Bring in some pots of herbs for windows.

Preparing the Soil

❧ Spread an inch of ripe compost on the surface of the garden and mix with the first four inches of soil.

❧ Use leaves and a thin layer of compost to mulch around perennials and newly planted seeds as soon as the ground freezes.

Grooming Flowers, Trees, and Shrubs

❧ Decide which perennials to leave in the garden for winter interest. Cut (not pull) the others level with the ground and compost the plant material.

- Plant bulbs in the ground.

- Plant bulbs in pots for forcing inside during the winter.

- Divide perennials.

- Plant seeds of hearty perennials and annuals to bloom for next spring.

- Plant new shrubs and trees (other than fruit trees).

- Compost grass, trees, and shrubs.

- Treat acid-loving plants with a fertilizer containing iron chelates.

- Dig up, dry, and store tubers and corms, which will not winter.

- Remove the annuals and vegetables by the roots and put the healthy ones on the compost heap.

- Pack soil and mulch around the feet of rosebushes.

MAINTENANCE

- Reseed bald spots in the lawn.

- Clean flowerpots, putting clay pots away so they won't be damaged.

- Rake and compost leaves.

- Gather twigs and sticks to use as kindling and store in baskets on the front porch where they will stay dry.

&. Clean up the garden shed and properly dispose of old chemicals.

&. Clean and oil implements, and prepare the lawn mower and grill for storage.

&. Store patio furniture.

&. Turn the compost and add a layer of fireplace ashes, bonemeal, dried blood, and dead leaves to the new soft green plant material. Dampen if necessary.

Exquisite Combinations of Spring Bulbs

Of all the jobs that must be done in the autumn, designing beds of spring-blooming bulbs is the most fun. The number of different arrangements you can create by bulb gardening is truly staggering, though you wouldn't know it from the rather ordinary combination of tulips, narcissi, crocus, and hyacinths growing in most spring gardens. Bulb planting takes time, work, and money. Yet, for some reason I've never understood, many gardeners rarely roam beyond red and yellow Darwin tulips and trumpet daffodils and fail to get the most out of their investment. Just think of the beautiful reward you'll get from spending a few minutes visiting a good nursery or reading its bulb catalog before you make your purchases. Pictures of the fringed-petal parrot tulips and daffodils; spider lilies with curved, ribbon petals; double-flowered peony tulips; or the gardenia-like blooms of the daffodil, *Narcissus "Acropolis,"* will melt the heart of anyone who has enough faith in nature to plant bulbs. Combining them with other types of bulbs like delicate wood anemones, sparkling blue scilla, tiny purple and white grape-like spikes of muscari, species crocus, and irises in pinks, blues, yellows, and white; and the smashing giant allium will give even the simplest garden a spectacular display of color from early March through June.

If I had but two loaves of bread, I would sell one and buy hyacinths, for they would feed my soul.

—The Koran

Suggestions for Bulb Plantings

STYLE

In autumn it's hard to envision how empty the landscape will be in spring. Masses of bulbs are needed to give the sense of a flower-filled space. A few lone daffodils call more attention to the emptiness than no daffodils at all. My trick is to figure out how many bulbs I need and then double it. This may seem extreme, but in the spring they never seem to look crowded. The look of a "full" garden is best achieved by planting in clusters—circles or triangles. Generally five to seven bulbs of the same color is the most effective way to plant larger varieties and ten to twelve for the smaller types. These patches of color bring a winter-weary perennial border back to life as early as the beginning of March. Another beautiful look can be achieved by planting whole beds in one color. Under a large flowering shrub I have such a bed about five feet by five feet that is filled with fiery red tulips in the spring and hosta in the summer.

Color

Mixed beds of primary colors—red, yellow, and purple: For a striking March-blooming planting try red tulips like kaufmanniana with early irises in yellow and violet.

Mixed beds of light and dark shades of one color: For an April-blooming pink planting try clusters of peony tulips like the shell pink "Angelique" combined with "Lilac Perfection." For a white to deep gold planting try creating a border with white muscari in the front, then yellow trout lilies, and the tall daffodil "Beau Monde" with white petals framing a gold cup in the back of a border.

With perennials: Early-blooming perennials and bulbs are natural companions. I can think of no better way to begin the spring than with wood anemones and hellebores. Beds of daylilies or hostas are excellent places to plant tulips. Their beautiful green foliage makes a perfect nest for colorful tulip heads. Lemon yellow and gold daffodils are striking with the yellow cat's-paw markings on pansies. The old-fashioned bleeding heart and late-blooming white daffodils as well as English primrose and grape hyacinths are stunning combinations. A favorite of mine is the cheerful little yellow celandine, which goes well with any early bulb.

Timing

Time the blooming period carefully. With small gardens careful planning of blooming is essential—especially when bulbs are planted with other flowers. In one front border I only have March-blooming bulbs, which will fade just in time to make room for the peonies. Where perennials aren't waiting in the wings, I stagger similar early and mid-season varieties for a continuous show until the end of May, when my attention begins to shift and I become engrossed in perennials. If bulbs are your favorites, or you haven't the opportunity to plant other flowers, a combination of late-blooming spring bulbs and lilies will carry your garden well into the summer.

Long as there's a sun that sets,
   Primroses will have their glory;
Long as there are violets,
   They will have a place in story:
There's a flower that shall be mine,
'Tis the little Celandine.
   —William Wordsworth, "To the Small Celandine"

In my garden grew plenty of thyme,
It would flourish by night and by day,
O'er the wall came a lad, he took all that I had,
   And stole my thyme away.
   —Michael Drayton, "Devonshire Song"

Lemony Walnut Bread

Lemon balm grows so rapidly I'm always looking for new ways to use it. This bread fills the house with its wonderful sweet smell.

Over a low flame heat just until dissolved three quarters cup of milk, one cup of sugar, one teaspoon of salt, and three tablespoons of vegetable oil. Remove immediately from heat. Pour the mixture into a large mixing bowl. When slightly cooled, add two slightly beaten eggs and stir. Sift together two cups of white flour, a half cup of whole-wheat flour, and three teaspoons of baking powder. Gradually stir the dry ingredients into the milk and egg. The batter should be thick but you should still be able to stir it. Add a quarter cup of very finely chopped lemon balm leaves, one and a half teaspoons of lemon extract, and three-quarters cup of ground walnuts. When the batter is smooth, pour into a buttered loaf pan. Bake in a preheated 350-degree oven for an hour or until the top is brown and a toothpick inserted comes out clean. Serve warm with butter.

Making a Compost Heap

No longer just a fad, composting is essential to reduce the waste clogging our landfills. Although anyone with a lawn should be composting, for gardeners it's also a way to maintain the fertility of their soil. Composting enables us to recycle yard and kitchen waste into natural fertilizer. Black gold—the glorious nutrient-rich organic material that fuels plant growth—is the amazing result of letting nature take her course. Almost any plant material will eventually turn into compost, but by following some simple steps you can rapidly accelerate the process.

Begin by building a container at least four feet square. Although you can buy a kit in garden centers, it's easy to make your own by driving four six-foot heavy metal garden stakes into the ground at each corner of the square. Fit a tough, thick piece of plastic or chicken wire about three feet high around it. The plastic or wire should fit snugly and the stakes must be very solid. A cover is helpful, but not necessary. Start with a layer of crisscrossed twigs and branches on the bottom about six inches thick. The twigs allow the air needed for decomposition to reach the bottom.

The material for composting should be separated into sources of carbon and nitrogen. Grass clippings are a nitrogen source—along with newly weeded or pruned green plants. The best source for carbon is dead leaves, cornstalks, and husks. Fireplace ashes also provide carbon, but they must be kept dry until they are used. Alternate layers of carbon and nitrogen material, using more carbon. Sprinkle a little topsoil between the layers and dampen (not soak!). A little dried blood, bonemeal, and aged manure can be added as you go to enrich the compost.

Lift and turn it periodically, mainly to get air in it. Normally, compost doesn't produce an odor, but if there is one, stirring it will eliminate it. The smaller the pieces of material the faster it will compost. No-nos in the compost heap include weeds that have gone to seed; tough, fibrous, or sticklike debris—like pine needles or branches; and food with any fat or oil.

Behold this compost! behold it well! . . .
The grass of spring covers the prairies,
The bean bursts noiselessly through the mould
   in the garden, . . .
The summer growth is innocent and disdainful above
   all those strata of sour dead. . . .
          —Walt Whitman, "This Compost"

8

In Due Time

In the second month the peach tree blooms, but not until the ninth
the chrysanthemums: so each must wait until his own time comes.

—ancient Chinese proverb

Michael and I looked at twenty-five houses before we first set eyes on the one that eventually became our home. Despite a gloomy spring rain, the house was set in the midst of an exquisite garden created by flowering shrubs and trees. That night as we compared the places we'd seen, I kept visualizing the delicate clouds of pastel blossoms surrounding the house. Although I can't explain why, it's important to me that this beauty comes from deep-rooted trees and shrubs, which are more enduring than flowers. David and Lisbe Elwyn, who transformed this simple yard into a garden many years before we moved here, understood that trees and shrubs become a part of a place.

Thanks to David and Lisbe's foresight, flowering shrubs bloom in our yard from the time the forsythia opens in early April well through June when the sweet jasmine scent of the mock orange bush finally fades away. Our neighbors' particular favorite is a rather ordinary spirea hedge in front of our house, which becomes quite regal when masses of stately long white spires announce that spring has truly arrived. As far as I'm concerned, life doesn't get much better than sitting on the front porch and inhaling the fragrance from the overblown white and purple lilac bushes—one on either side of the front yard—when they burst into bloom in May.

In the backyard numerous bright orange, pink, and white tree azaleas and deep pink and white rhododendrons form the spine of a long flowering shrub border that is chock-full of naturalized daffodils. A few years ago one of David and Lisbe's redbuds became too large for its space in the side yard and I moved it to the backyard border. The next year it grew a foot in every direction as if to say, "Finally, I can stretch my legs." As I looked at the redbud I realized something was missing— a dogwood. The two trees bring the Indiana hills to life in the spring, and I was aching to see a dogwood outside my window. The following autumn I planted the largest pink dogwood tree I could find. Since then I've added flowering plum and peach trees, a red-twigged dogwood, tree peonies, butterfly bushes, and many varieties of rhododendrons, azaleas, and hydrangeas. Although all of these have been assets to the garden from the beginning, I love them most of all because they are my lasting contribution, my stamp on this place where I've worked so hard and long. Ten or fifteen years from now someone may look back to me as I look to the Elwyns and say, thank you for giving us these beautiful trees.

Those that come after me will gather these roses,
And watch, as I do now, the white wisteria
Burst, in the sunshine, from its pale green sheath.

Planned. Planted. Established. Then neglected,
Till at last the loiterer by the gate will wonder
At the old, old cottage, the old wooden cottage,
And say, "One might build here, the view is glorious;
This must have been a pretty garden once."
                              —Mary Ursula Bethell, "Time"

Wisdom from
Mamaw Tribby's Garden

Last night, there came a frost, which has done great damage to my garden. . . . It is sad that Nature will play such tricks with us poor mortals, inviting us with sunny smiles to confide in her, and then, when we are entirely within her power, striking us to the heart.
                                                    —Nathaniel Hawthorne

When I was a girl it was my job to rake leaves in the fall, just about the time school started, bringing with it activities much more interesting than leaf raking. I postponed the chore time and again—until it was too late. Big, dry flakes of snow started falling early in November one year and didn't stop until over a foot had accumulated. This severe weather continued every weekend throughout the autumn. All winter I looked out on a yard encrusted with caked and soggy leaves caused by my procrastination.

   Mamaw Tribby said this experience should teach me one of the most important lessons a gardener can learn—nature waits for no one. We think we can control her, but all we can do is follow her lead. As we puttered in her flower beds, she'd say, "People are in awe of nature when they first start gardening and follow all the rules. The trouble starts when they get cocky and think they can do things at their own convenience."

Nature takes no account of even the
most reasonable of human excuses.
                              —Joseph Wood Krutch

Lessons
from the
Gardener's Journal

The Garden's Workhorses

> Loveliest of trees, the cherry now
> Is hung with bloom along the bough.
> —A. E. Housman, "A Shropshire Lad"

From the dining room window we are greeted by the sight of a weeping winter cherry tree in the yard of our neighbor and friend Joyce Dopkeen. It's lovely throughout the year, but unforgettable in the spring when its long elegant branches arch to the ground as if weighted down by an impossibly light and fragile cloud of tiny pinkish white flowers. Flowering shrubs and ornamental trees, like Joyce's weeping cherry, are the workhorses of the garden. Technically, a shrub is any woody stemmed plant. They are closely related to trees as well as woody stemmed vines, like clematis and wisteria, which climb on a solid vertical surface. Generally a shrub becomes a tree when it has a single trunk and grows to heights of fourteen feet or more. The word *shrub* evokes little charm and does little to make this category of extraordinarily useful plants more appealing. How unfortunate! No other species contributes so much for so little in return. It's a wise gardener who carves time from a busy October gardening schedule to make a place for them.

Regardless of the season, shrubs enhance the beauty of the garden. Most have spectacular periods of blooming beginning with the earliest true flower found in most cold climates, the yellow-petaled Chinese witch hazel. Then the forsythia buds open, and around here the roadsides and walkways scream "yellow." In rapid succession an extraordinary array of ornamental trees and shrubs stagger blooming periods all the way through late summer. If you're careful to deadhead its spent blooms, the butterfly bush will keep producing long graceful rose or lavender spires until the pink heather and white cones of hydrangea paniculata are at their peak in September.

As if magnificent floral displays weren't enough, many of these plants return to the limelight in late autumn with berries and bright foliage. An excellent and unusual choice for this purpose is butcher's broom, which produces extraordinary berries for holiday decorations. Even in the dead of winter, shrubs like the spike winterhazel, the exotic "Harry Lauder's Walking Stick," or another favorite of mine, the tree azalea, make dramatic sculptural forms against a barren earth. Vibrant color from the stems of a red-twigged dogwood or coral embers willow also enlivens the drab winter landscape.

For all of this you need only to plant in October when the soil is still warm, do a little pruning, or with some species like rhododendron, water during droughts, add a handful of fertilizer in the fall, and watch them perform. What I most appreciate about them isn't the flowers they produce—though the blooming of hydrangeas, lilacs, and azaleas is as glorious as any event in the garden—but the sense of endurance that shrubs and small trees create. A magnolia tree nestled in a bed of pachysandra or even in the middle of the lawn provides instant structure to an entire section of the garden. Add a little stone path leading to a wooden bench in the shade of the magnolia, some moss pinks peeking around the stones, and you have a delightful and long-lasting source of pleasure. Even if you don't have the time to walk up the path, sit on the bench, and absorb the mysteries of nature, a quick glance from your kitchen window and your mind will take you there.

> And in the woods a fragrance rare
> Of wild azaleas fills the air,
> And richly tangled overhead
> We see their blossoms sweet and red.
> —Dora Read Goodale,
>   "Spring Scatters Far and Wide"

Selecting the Perfect Flowering Shrub or Tree

What if you have seen it before, ten thousand times over? An apple tree in full blossom is like a message, sent fresh from heaven to earth, of purity and beauty!

—Henry Ward Beecher

Finding the right shrub or ornamental tree for your needs and placing it in a spot where it will thrive and give you many years of pleasure requires careful thought. The first step is to determine what is most important to you: exquisite flowers; an especially long-lasting blooming period; autumn or winter interest; a bushy, dense habitat for privacy; fast growth; etc. A few plants will meet two or three of your goals, but in most cases, the best specimens for any one purpose aren't the most versatile.

After you determine your priorities, look at the catalogs of nurseries that carry a large selection so you can also consider the less common choices. Now think about the aesthetics—color, shape, size. Next, look at your site. Shrubs and ornamental trees are the garden's stay-at-homes. Once they are in place, they really don't like to be moved, so the amount of sun, water, and wind and type of soil must be suitable. Many people don't think of wind, but some plants like the tree peony must be protected from wind, while "Harry Lauder's Walking Stick" prefers it. At this point, you've eliminated many wonderful plants that aren't appropriate for you and focused on five or six choices. If at all possible, go to a botanical garden and see fully grown specimens in a real setting. Now, go with your heart. Pick the one you love the most.

The Most Spectacular Flowering Shrubs

Plant	Color	Shape/Size	Leaf	Sun/Shade	Soil/Water	Zones
TREE PEONY *Comments:* the most beautiful shrub known	Glorious huge flowers in white, yellow, pink to scarlet	Bushy foliage on 4–5' knotty trunk	Deciduous	Full sun to some shade	Medium weight and neutral soil	4–8
VIBURNUM *Comments:* beautiful from spring through fall	Pink buds form highly fragrant white flowers	Bushy; grows to 15'	Deciduous; lovely autumn foliage and berries	Sun	Moderately rich and well drained	5–8
GARLAND DAPHNE *Comments:* one of the best plants for rock gardens	Fragrant rose pink flowers in May; "alba" is a white variety	2' wide and 9–12" high; compact and rounded	Evergreen; narrow dark lustrous leaves	Sun to some shade	Well-drained, moist, neutral soil; don't move after established	4–8

Where Summer Flowering Is the Most Important Consideration

Plant	Color	Shape/Size	Leaf	Sun/Shade	Soil/Water	Zones
BUTTER-FLY BUSH Comments: also called summer lilac	White, pinks, purple; dead-head flowers to prolong blooming	Shaggy bush grows to 16'+; prune heavily in spring	Deciduous	Full sun in colder areas but tolerates some shade where warmer	Hearty, prefers well-drained soil but will grow anywhere	6–8
MOUNTAIN LAUREL Comments: wild in Northeast but is a protected species—buy in nursery	Natives are pink or white but new cultivars are deeper pinks and red	Grows to 6–8'; rounded shape	Evergreen; looks like rhododendron	Sun to partial shade; won't bloom in full shade	Peaty, moist, well-drained acidic soil; plant with part of the root ball above ground and mulch well	4–8
LAVENDER Comments: dried for sachets; used as ground cover or hedge	Mauve to deep purple spires	Grows to 3' in compact rounded bushes	Evergreen, especially in warmer climates; cut back heavily after flowering	Sun	Tolerates poor soil, as long as well drained	5–8

WHERE AUTUMN COLOR IS THE MOST IMPORTANT CONSIDERATION

Plant	Color	Shape/Size	Leaf	Sun/Shade	Soil/Water	Zones
SUMMER-SWEET OR CLETHRA "ROSEA" Comments: fragrant flowers	Deep pink buds; pink flowers in late summer and deep orange fall foliage	4–6' height	Deciduous	Full sun for best color	Slightly acidic, moist, sandy soil	3–9
SHAD-BUSH OR AMELAN-CHIER Comments: dramatic	White flowers in spring; scarlet in autumn	8' bushes	Deciduous; bluish-green summer foliage	Full sun for the best autumn display	Slightly acidic, moist, but well-drained soil	4–8
CHOKE-BERRY OR ARONIA Comments: requires almost no care	White flowers in spring; scarlet leaves and berries in autumn	Bushy 9' tall to 5' wide	Deciduous	Sun to partial shade	Hearty; keep moist in well-drained soil	5–8

WHERE WINTER COLOR OR FORM IS THE MOST IMPORTANT CONSIDERATION

Plant	Color	Shape/Size	Leaf	Sun/Shade	Soil/Water	Zones
CORYLUS AVELLANA "CONTORTA" *Comments:* also called Harry Lauder's Walking Stick	Long pendulous catkins turn yellow in winter	Can reach 8' with corkscrew branches used in floral arrangements	Deciduous	Either	Hearty; loamy soil	3–8
FRAGRANT WINTERSWEET OR CHIMONANTHUS PRAECOX *Comments:* sweet smell	Translucent yellow flowers with red centers blooming at New Year's	Grows to 10–12' tall and 8' wide	Deciduous; turning lovely ocher in autumn	Partial shade	Well-drained soil enriched with humus; needs regular watering	6–9
CORAL EMBERS WILLOW; OR SALIX ALBA "BRITZENSIS" *Comments:* easy to grow for dramatic results	Primary color is from bright red stems in winter from new growth; prune hard in late winter for color	Grows about 5' every year	Deciduous; leaves turn attractive yellow in autumn	Sun to partial sun	Hearty; prefers well-drained soil but will do well in wet soil—good choice where drainage is poor	2–8

Secrets of Successful Planting

After you've chosen your location, make sure that your site meets the requirements of the plant and check the soil and drainage. Heavy clay soil and poor drainage are frequently the culprit when a plant fails in the first year. Check the drainage of the spot you've selected by seeing how well water drains after a rainfall. If the water seems to remain standing, wait a while for the ground to dry a bit, then dig a hole, fill it with water, and see how long it takes to drain. If it hasn't completely drained in an hour, loosen the soil underneath the hole and see if it drains. If water is still standing, try to find another location. If that isn't possible, dig a hole wider than normal and leave the top of the root ball slightly above the soil line. Cover it with soil and mulch.

Be very careful to keep all newly planted shrubs and trees well watered for the first year. They don't have the roots that enable them to drink deeply like established shrubs and trees, so they depend on surface water. If nature doesn't provide it, you must! Failure to water trees is a common reason for their loss. The most effective way to water for a large planting project is a soaker hose. If you don't use one, make sure you completely saturate the root ball to its base when you water.

Prepare the site by removing the sod and breaking and turning the soil. If you have rocks, this can be quite a challenge. When I lived in Stone Ridge, New York, and uncovered giant slabs of bluestone every time I wanted to plant, I discovered a pick, shovel, and strong back are essential. On these occasions you may need help! After the rocks are removed, loosen the soil at least three feet around the root ball. Remember, the harder it is for you to spade the soil, the harder it will be for the delicate roots to push through. The hole itself should have straight sides and be at least twice the size of the root ball. Make certain that the soil underneath isn't disturbed. This can cause the root ball to settle too low in the hole and cause crown rot, a fatal problem that especially afflicts evergreens. Loosen the surrounding soil and remove about half of it. Add peat moss or compost and work it in. These additives provide more nutrients for the plant and an absorbent medium to help hold moisture in dry periods.

Before removing the shrub from its container, make sure that the root ball is moist. Next, turn the shrub upside down and tap it to loosen it or cut the side of the container if it is too large to invert. Examine the roots and if any are dead, remove them. Also prune the plant back about a third of its growth, removing any dead wood. If the root ball is packed in burlap, cut any wires or rope and fold back the top of the cover but don't remove. Plant the root ball at the same level that the nursery planted it. Fill in around the root ball with alternating layers of soil and soil mixed with peat or compost. When finished, encircle the plant in a trough about two to three feet out, depending on the plant's size. This is to help trap water. Mulch and water.

Come, let us plant the apple-tree.
Cleave the tough greensward with the spade;
Wide let its hollow bed be made;
There gently lay the roots, and there
Sift the dark mould with kindly care.
— William Cullen Bryant,
"The Planting of the Apple-Tree"

Topsy-Turvy Cherry Torte

> Those cherries fairly do enclose
> Of orient pearl a double row,
> Which when her lovely laughter shows,
> They look like rosebuds filled with snow.
> —Thomas Campion, *Fourth Book of Airs*

When the temperatures begin to drop and your body begins to crave something sweet to ward off the chills, this old-fashioned cake is a welcome treat. If you are lucky enough to have a cherry tree, this is a wonderful use for the fresh fruit, but canned cherries can be substituted. Use tart pitted cherries, not a prepared pie filling.

Use a no-stick nine-by-nine-inch cake pan. Melt four tablespoons of butter with a third of a cup of dark rum and a half cup of sugar. Add two cups of pitted cherries. If you use canned cherries, drain all but a quarter cup of the syrup. Stir gently, being careful not to mash the cherries. Taste, and if the cherries are tart, add more sugar, as desired. When mixed, pour over the bottom of the pan so the cherries are evenly distributed. Make the following batter and spread over the cherries.

Measure two cups of flour and sift together with two and a half teaspoons of baking powder and a quarter teaspoon of salt. Sift again. Cream together one cup of sugar and a third of a cup of butter until fluffy. Separate two eggs, beat the yolks, and add to the butter and sugar mixture. Beat well. Begin adding the flour mixture, alternating with one and a quarter cups of light cream. Beat the egg whites until stiff, adding a pinch of cream of tartar. Fold into the batter. Bake at 350 degrees for fifty minutes or until the cake is brown on top and done when tested with a toothpick. Use a knife to loosen the cake from the sides of the pan and invert the pan on a platter. Serve warm with sweetened whipped cream. A low-cholesterol version of this cake is also delicious. Just substitute one cup of enriched nonfat milk for the light cream, margarine for the butter, and a half cup frozen egg substitute, thawed, for the egg yolks.

Making an Autumn Wreath

I started making my own wreaths years ago when I realized vines hanging from trees in the woods were all I needed to get started. Since then, I've discovered that odds and ends from the garden and woods can be transformed into unique and beautiful accents for the house and yard. In addition to the usual wreath on the front door, I like to place them on the patio and the garden shed. Cut six woody vines like grapevines into six-foot lengths and loop them into one big circle about one and a half to two inches in diameter. Wrap a smaller piece of the same type of vine every few inches to secure the circle and tuck the end in the vines. Do this one or two more times until the wreath feels secure. Tuck about ten individual pieces of bittersweet, each on a three- or four-inch branch, into the wreath at even intervals. Add six to eight dried hydrangeas of equal size. Using florist wire, attach six or seven ears of miniature dried Indian corn with purplish dried husks. Spread open the husks. Dried orange and purple straw flowers or statice can be added for a fuller look. Push the stems into the wreath so only the flower head shows. Use florist wire to make a hook and attach to the door with a suction-cup wreath holder available in craft stores.

> I sent thee late a rosy wreath . . .
> But thou thereon didst only breathe,
> And sent'st back to me. . . .
> —Ben Jonson, "To Celia"

9

The Journey Home

All things on earth point home in old October. . . .
—Thomas Wolfe, *Of Time and the River*

Tears, idle tears, I know not what they mean . . .
Rise in the heart, and gather to the eyes,
In looking on the happy autumn fields,
And thinking of the days that are no more.
—Alfred, Lord Tennyson, "Tears, Idle Tears"

Despite the many beautiful autumns of my childhood, the fall when Mother was dying of breast cancer is the one I remember most vividly. I was a confused and sad teenager, trying to understand why this was happening to *my* mother—who was so loved and needed by all of us. As I trudged through the fallen leaves in the woods after school, her fight for life seemed to be reflected in the fire-lit world around me. Golden hickories and oaks soared over thickets of persimmon trees, sassafras, and dogwoods blooming in every red from salmon pink to crimson. Winter nipped at my heels as I struggled to understand life and the cycle of the seasons.

In the mornings a thick haze settled in the hills, and at sunrise I saw fingers of pink mist crawling over the fields from my bedroom window. I believed in heaven because I figured it looked a lot like the farm on those autumn mornings, but it didn't make this time any easier or my pain any less. Mother eventually died in November, though not for several more years. From that first autumn when I knew she would leave us one day much too soon, my spirits always fell along with the leaves and did not perk up until winter.

When I began to garden I found that this seasonal depression diminished—especially if I had flowers blooming in October to remind me of the happiness yet to come in my life. Prolonging the growing season became a passion of mine. As long as the days were still warm I couldn't bear to look out on beds and borders populated with only a few defiant roses. Mums were never a favorite of mine but I was too inexperienced to know how to keep my October garden flourishing without them. Then I planted a couple of large decorative dahlias. Like most beginning gardeners, my taste in flowers wasn't subtle, but I was hardly prepared for the masses of bold, bright flowers these two stringy little tubers produced. When I saw their giant scarlet heads laughing in the face of winter, my mood began to soar. My first obsession with a particular flower was born. I later learned that many experts find the dahlia gaudy and stiff, but to me it's both passionate and elegant. From July until the first frost the pure vitality these majestic flowers brought to my garden helped me outgrow the sadness I felt at this time of year. It's strange to think that growing a flower could be so healing, but my dahlias helped me to remember the joy Mother gave. Since then, I've come to value the hard lesson I learned so long ago about the fleeting nature of life. I know the secret is to enjoy what we have rather than dwelling on what we've lost—and never have a garden without dahlias.

Nothing in this world is really precious until we know that it will soon be gone.

—Donald Culross Peatrie, *An Almanac for Moderns*

Wisdom from
Mamaw Tribby's Garden

At twilight in the garden
And, I am working here all alone
In my heart there comes a longing . . .
To know you're coming home.
　　—Mamaw Tribby, "In Memory of Bill," 1950

Even as a child I was struck by the clear blue of the October sky. While we mulched flowers, Mamaw Tribby often said the sky came very close to the earth to protect the garden so the roots could make the journey home. When I asked her where the flowers went, she always said the same thing: "To spend the winter with your Grandpaw Bill, the best gardener I ever knew. They are tired now, but in the spring when they return they'll be rested and more beautiful than ever."

　　Mamaw Tribby knew she could not escape the economic hardships, the illness and death that were so much a part of farming, but my grandfather's death left an emptiness in her life she never could fill. Although he was eighteen years her senior, they were each other's closest companion and dearest friend. He died the summer before I was born, but his presence was always with us when we were working in the garden. As she puttered among her flowers and remembered a long-forgotten joke they had once shared, I could see her accept the pain as well as the joy of life. She taught her grandchildren that both are a part of a divine plan. She would tell us, "See how gracefully the rose gives up its petals to make way for rosebuds in the spring."

In my Autumn garden I was fain
To mourn among my scattered roses;
Alas for that last rosebud that uncloses
To Autumn's languid sun and rain. . . .
—Christina Rossetti, "An October Garden"

Lessons from the Gardener's Journal

A Second Spring

> Doesn't it seem as if autumn were the real creator,
> more creative than spring . . . ?
> —Rainer Maria Rilke

Chrysanthemums in white or earth tones seem to be the only potted plants found late in the growing season when most gardeners are ready to put their garden to bed and go apple picking. Yet, with just a bit of research in nursery catalogs or a midseason visit to a good garden center, you'll discover numerous varieties of flowers that peak from late August through early November—or even longer depending on the weather and your location. Every year my list of autumn-blooming flowers and shrubs gets longer and more varied. Although there are a fair number of golds and reds, I always seem to choose the pinks and purples. Blue is a rarity in the fall, and the only pure blue flower I've had success with is monkshood with its delphinium-like spires. Few flowers, though, can compete with the showy ten-inch blooms of the perennial hibiscus Rose Mallow, which can be found in lovely shades of pink and red. I have a deep red "Lord Baltimore" at the front walkway, which causes quite a stir among passersby from August until the first frost. Sedum is always a good choice, and "Autumn Joy," a mainstay of the late-blooming garden, attracts butterflies throughout the fall. This tall, versatile plant is especially beautiful planted in beds with asters like the densely flowered "Purple Dome" or "Frikartii" and artemisia "Ludoviciana" with its broad, whitish leaves. Bulbs should not be forgotten. Snowdrop anemones first open in May but have a repeat performance in the fall at the same time the delicate lavender crocus blooms. Right at the top of the list of spectacular fall bloomers is the butterfly bush. Last summer I planted on the side of the front porch a "Pink Delight," with long stems bearing large spiked pink flowers. What a success—especially with the monarch butterflies who visited it daily.

I've always thought of the hydrangea as the aristocrat of autumn. By late September and October, the Hydrangea Paniculata "grandiflora" growing beside the garage is gracefully weighted down by opulent white flowers that mellow into the color of old linen. On the north side of the house the summer-blooming pink and blue flowers of the "Macrophylla" cultivars have dried to the color of sea foam—proving that nothing in nature fades as artfully as the hydrangea. Right after the first mild frost, I gather bunches for giant arrangements that will last well into the winter to remind me of the garden's autumn generosity.

The autumn wood the aster knows,
The empty nest, the wind that grieves,
The sunlight breaking thro' the shade,
The squirrel chattering overhead,
The timid rabbits lighter tread
Among the rustling leaves.
            —Dora Read Goodale

Fall-Blooming Flowers for the Second Spring

Asters "New England": Numerous varieties, most blooming through September. The pink "Kessel" flourishes through October.

Chrysanthemums: Keep buds pinched off until July 4 for autumn blooming.

Cimicifuga "White Pearl": A tall plant also called fairy candles with lovely white flowers on lacy foliage through October.

Dahlias: Enormous range of flowers that bloom from midsummer until frost in every color but blue.

Dianthus "Doris": Fragrant pink flounced edges with a darker center blooming until the first frost.

Helenium "Autumnal Brilliant": Stunning rust orange flowers from the end of August to October.

Hibiscus "Lord Baltimore" and "Southern Belle": Dramatic giant flowers more tolerant to the cold than other hibiscus—but they do require moist soil.

Malva "Alcea Fastigiata": Like its relative the hollyhock, sports dainty pink blooms through October.

Pansies: Use the medium-sized flowers for color until frost and, unlike the larger varieties, they'll produce a nice display the following spring.

Phlox Carolina "Rosalinda" and P. Decussata "Franz Schubert": Both lilac pinks that bloom through September.

Physostegia: Tall pink or white spikes that bloom in late summer and early autumn.

Rudbeckia: Hardy golden daisylike flowers that bloom from July through October and provide interesting seed pods for the winter garden.

Sedum "Autumn Joy": Showy pinkish flower heads that fade to a deep rust make this one of the most dependable and useful of autumn bloomers.

Season of mists and mellow fruitfulness!
—John Keats, "Ode to Autumn"

Growing Great Dahlias

Few species of flowers are as diverse as the dahlia—from small bedding plants to giant "dinnerplate" flowers in shapes from pompoms to starfish. I'm most partial to the giant cactus-flowered dahlias with long, narrow, pointed, incurling petals and the delicate collarettes in wildly exotic color combinations, like the maroon, white, and gold "Awaikoe." Dahlias are easy to care for. These steps will give you masses of breathtaking flowers from late summer until frost.

Oh, little rose tree, bloom!
Summer is nearly over.
The dahlias bleed, and the phlox is seed.
Nothing's left of the clover.
—Edna St. Vincent Millay,
song from "The Lamp and the Bell"

THE SITE

Although dahlias are not temperamental, the site is especially important in growing them successfully. When they are planted in a sunny, open location protected from harsh winds in a well-drained, loose, rich soil and not allowed to dry, they'll bloom profusely. The roots must be permitted to spread out freely. If your ground is heavy, mix peat moss or sand with the topsoil. Aged manure or compost and bonemeal can be worked into the soil at the end of the growing season to improve it.

PLANTING

Dahlias are very sensitive to frost—wait at least two weeks after the frost date for your area to plant. I usually set them out the first week of June. After several years of trying to turn full-grown dahlias toward the patio so the faces were visible, I learned that dahlias will persistently face the sun. You'll get more pleasure from them if they are planted so you can see them. When you open a package you'll find a mass of roots and tubers; take care, as the tubers are delicate. Gently unravel them to identify the individual tubers for planting. Position each tuber "eyes up" with the top of the tuber about three inches from the surface of the soil. The spacing will depend on the type of dahlia you are planting. With other flowers I often plant more closely than the nursery recommends, but with dahlias I scrupulously follow directions and may even leave extra space for very large varieties.

PRUNING

One of the least attractive features of dahlias is their tendency to become leggy. If unchecked, they can create a miniature rain forest in your flower bed. I grow only six or seven stems from each tuber. Exhibitors often grow only one stem. As new ones emerge, cut them back. After several leaves have fully developed on each of the stems, pinch new growth back to encourage more foliage. One of the reasons I love dahlias is that they are wonderful in bouquets, but they often produce a huge flower on a tiny stem—quite a challenge to the flower arranger. If you remove the two smaller side buds that typically accompany the primary bud, the stem will be lengthened and the flower will be even bigger and more showy. As the season progresses, remove the spent blooms to prolong flowering.

FEEDING AND WATERING

Dahlias should be fed but only on the surface, with a fertilizer high in phosphate and low in nitrogen, during the growing and flowering period. Nitrogen will encourage wild foliage growth but not promote more flowers. Feed when you first cut back the stems, a second time when the first buds appear, and then about once a month. If you plan to overwinter the tubers, stop feeding in early October. Dahlias do not like dry soil and should be mulched to help them retain their moisture. Give them a heavy soaking weekly with tepid water except in rainy periods. I leave a long hose filled with water in the sun for this purpose.

STAKING AND STORING

Once dahlias start growing they shoot up like teenagers. For this reason many people stake them as soon as they are planted. I prefer to wait until it's necessary, only because the bare stakes can be so ugly. Whichever method you choose, you'll need to be careful not to damage the roots, especially with the large varieties, which require very heavy stakes. When the frost has turned the foliage and flowers black, it's time to cut the foliage off to about three inches above the soil. Leave the tuber in the ground another week to ten days unless a hard frost is predicted. For storage, shake the soil off and divide into large clumps, making sure that each has an eye or bud from which a stem will grow. Dip the cuts in powdered sulfur and store them in flat cardboard boxes filled with a commercial mix used to grow seedlings, peat moss, or sawdust. The hardest part about storing tubers is keeping them above freezing, but cool enough to stop growth (up to forty-five degrees), all the while maintaining a slightly damp environment. When they are too wet, they rot; too dry, and they shrivel. Look at them occasionally and cut out any bad spots. Although Mamaw Tribby would be appalled to hear me suggest this, if the storage is more than you can manage, just discard the tubers and treat dahlias like annuals. They're still one of the best bargains in the garden.

Dividing Perennials

Dividing perennials is a backbreaking and dirty chore, but essential if you want a thriving flower bed. The specific guidelines for division differ from plant to plant, so you'll need to do a little research before digging in. Some such as lupines or bleeding heart cannot tolerate division, while others like peonies, rose mallow, and daylilies can be divided but usually don't need to be. Rudbeckia, bee balm, yarrow, coreopsis, mums, helenium autumnal, or bearded irises are among those plants that must be divided every few years and in a few cases—asters come to mind—every year or two. Important signs will tell you when you shouldn't put the job off any longer are: The plant produces foliage but few blooms, or an empty spot emerges in the middle of a large established plant. In some cases, you may want to restrict unattractive or unwanted growth, while in others you may want to propagate a specific plant. Not all perennials can be increased by division, but for those that can, it's the natural way to expand your garden.

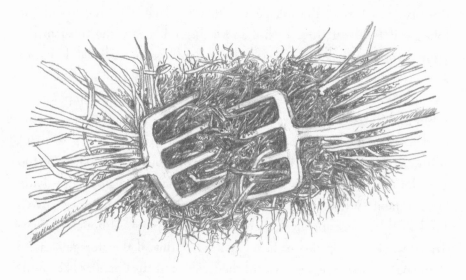

Some flowers are best divided in the spring, but others can be divided in the autumn. In either case the work should be finished early in the season. I aim for two months before the onset of severe weather—hot or cold. However, there's no substitute for following the specific division instructions for each plant. And, remember, most perennials that can be divided will survive regardless of when you do it to them—at worst you'll lose a blooming season. For example, bearded irises should be divided when they go into a short period of dormancy right after they bloom. One autumn we were having construction done, which required moving a whole bed. I decided if they had to be disturbed, I'd take this as an opportunity to divide them. The following spring about half of them didn't bloom but all survived, and the next year they were all more stunning than ever.

Plants that grow in clumps should be lifted from the earth by inserting your shovel far enough away to include most of the root system. This can be very difficult. Using a heavy old butcher knife, small handsaw, or spade, cut the clump into sections. Try to cut *between* the stems. If the clump is too large to lift, use a pitchfork or spade to break the mass of roots into sections. Transplant the divisions as soon as possible and water immediately. If the weather is still hot, cover the transplants with a folded newspaper or old umbrella. If you can't transplant that same day, soak the roots in a tub of water. Sometimes unforeseen events occur and planting has to be delayed. If you keep the roots wet, certain hearty plants will live in water quite a while, but you're taking a chance.

Wilted Spinach and Basil Salad

Tarragon is cherished in gardens. . . . Ruellius and such others have reported many strange tales hereof scarce worth the noting, saying that the seede of flaxe put into a radish roote or sea onion, and so set, doth bring forth this herbe Tarragon.

—Parkinson, *Paradisus terrestris,* 1629

This is a wonderful salad to make when you want to use the last of the fresh herbs in the garden. Although I prefer it with basil, other sweet herbs can be substituted.

Fill a large salad bowl with eight to ten cups of cleaned and torn spinach leaves, five chopped scallions, including the tender green stalks, a half cup of fresh chopped basil, and two sweet oranges in sections.

Heat five ounces of fresh mushrooms, sliced, with one tablespoon of butter. Add a quarter cup of thawed orange juice concentrate. Simmer over a low flame for one minute.

Make a salad dressing by stirring a third of a cup of olive oil with a third of a cup of sweet white balsamic vinegar or rice wine vinegar. Add one chopped scallion, salt and pepper to taste, and stir. Add the salad dressing to the mushrooms and bring to a complete boil. Let it simmer gently for one or two minutes. Pour the dressing over the spinach and oranges and invert the skillet over the bowl for five minute to let the spinach wilt. Sprinkle with fresh ground black pepper and toss before serving. Shaved pecorino Romano cheese can be added to each serving, if desired.

Brewing Herbal Teas

> My garden grew Self-heal and Balm,
> And Speedwell that's blue for an hour,
> Then blossoms again, O, grievous my pain,
> I'm plundered of each flower.
> —Michael Drayton, "Devonshire Song"

I know autumn has arrived when we stop spending the evenings on the patio with ice tea and begin drinking hot tea in front of a fire in the living room. A cup of fresh herbal tea made from the last of the herbs in the garden is a wonderful way to relax after a long day. Many herbs are quite hardy and thrive well beyond the first frosts. Lemon balm is my favorite, but other herbs I like to brew are mint, rosemary, feverfew, evening primrose, dill, and marigold leaves. Just pick a tablespoon of herbs for each cup and one "for the pot." Wash and cut into pieces with scissors. Rinse out a teapot with hot water. Place the herbs in a tea ball, which you put in the pot. Fill the pot with fresh boiling water. Steep for ten minutes.

Drying herbs for teas and cooking is also very easy. Cut branches with leaves attached. Although purists say the peak of flavor is before the herb has flowered, I've never been able to tell the difference. Most herbs are very cooperative and can be picked at any time. Tie them together and hang the bundles upside down in a cool, dry space. After they have dried thoroughly, remove the leaves from the branches without crushing them. Store in a glass jar with a tight lid or a plastic freezer bag. In a cool pantry they'll keep until you have a supply of fresh herbs in the spring.

Winter

The Stillness

> . . . the whited air
> Hides hills and woods, the river, and the heaven,
> And veils the farm-house at the garden's end. . . .
> —Ralph Waldo Emerson, "The Snow-Storm"

10

A Holiday Garden

From our snug fireside this Christmas-tide
We'll keep old Winter out.
—Thomas Noel, "Old Winter"

Traditions are what make the holidays special, but I discovered even greater meaning in letting one go. We are blessed to have a wonderful, old house—very formal with high ceilings and an ornate fireplace—that lends itself to traditional Christmas decorations. One of the highlights of my year is the ritual of decorating it for the holidays. Sometime during the first week in December I retrieve the holiday curtains from the attic and drape them with long ropes of evergreens at each window. The heavy crimson swags are festive against the yellow walls of the living and dining rooms. I twist more evergreen rope through the staircase railings with their beautiful turned volutes. Pine cones, along with bittersweet left over from Thanksgiving, and trinkets accumulated over the years embellish the evergreen ropes on the stairs. Tiny poinsettias on each step create a celebration of red. The house is alive with the colors of amaryllis, red cyclamen, and Christmas cactus, and the outside doors each have a traditional evergreen wreath. The crowning jewel is the Christmas tree, which fills a corner of the living room, but last year for the first time in my life, our tree was artificial.

One of my most cherished childhood memories is going to the woods with Daddy to cut the tree and then decorating it with popcorn ropes and ornaments. Back then I always thought that each tree was happy to be chosen, but now I question whether it's right to cart living trees from their forest homes to sell on concrete lots. As the holidays approach, I am torn between my warm recollections from childhood and the sad fate of the trees. Finally last year I decided that my respect for nature couldn't take a backseat to having a tastefully decorated house, and we came home with a fake Douglas fir. We decorated it with all the ornaments accumulated through our marriage—the painted papier-mâché balls from England, the fleur-de-lis from Quebec City, and delicate glass swans that were Mother's. From the garden I brought in sprays of dried branches of crabapple and hydrangea to nestle between the boughs. Despite my fears, it was truly beautiful. As I looked at it and thought about January's sad accumulation of tree skeletons, I decided it was the most beautiful I'd ever had.

The walls and ceiling were so hung with living green, that it looked a perfect grove, from every part of which, bright gleaming berries glistened. The crisp leaves of holly, mistletoe, and ivy reflected back the light, as if so many little mirrors had been scattered there; and such a mighty blaze went roaring up the chimney, as that dull petrifaction of a hearth had never known in Scrooge's time. . . .

—Charles Dickens, *A Christmas Carol*

Wisdom from
Mamaw Tribby's Garden

Rings and jewels are not gifts, but apologies for gifts.
The only gift is a portion of thyself.
—Ralph Waldo Emerson, *Essays,* Second Series: "Gifts"

As a child I learned to appreciate whatever gifts we were fortunate enough to get. When I was about nine I had begged Santa every night for weeks to bring me a particular doll that I had set my heart on. Christmas morning arrived and my brothers, sister, and I ran down the stairs to see what treasure had been left for us under the tree. After a frantic search beneath the tree I found not my doll but a different one—a wholly unacceptable replacement that could only be intended for me. I tried not to show my feelings while we unwrapped gifts and everyone else happily tinkered with new toys or tried on clothes to see if they fit. Mother called me into the kitchen where she was making breakfast. She didn't say that the doll I wanted was too expensive and Daddy had a bad year on the farm. I knew that anyway. Instead she reminisced about a Christmas long ago when she was about my age. In those days money was especially scarce. Often Mamaw Tribby could give Mother and her brothers and sisters only things she had made or grown in her garden. This particular year Mamaw Tribby's gift to Mother was a dried bouquet of beautiful red roses. She had written Mother a little poem, now long lost, that said these roses will crumble and return to the earth but the mother's love that brings them will last forever. After listening to Mother's story, I looked at my new doll and decided it was perfect.

Gifts tied with silver ribbon, son
Are prized the whole world over.
But, through the years, I remember
The scent of fragrant crumbled clover.
   —Mamaw Tribby, "Gifts"

Lessons
from the
Gardener's Journal

Evergreens and Lights

As a child I always felt a little cheated because my birthday, December 22, sometimes seemed lost in the flurry of Christmas celebrations. Yet, when I grew older, I learned to appreciate its timing because it marks one of the most auspicious events in nature. The 22nd is the first day after the shortest of the year—the winter solstice—when the days begin to lengthen. Like many children, I was fascinated with ancient man and could imagine how terrifying long, desolate, dark winters must have been to our ancestors. I thought of what it would be like to see everything on earth wither and die—except the evergreen—not knowing that the sun would come back in the spring and make the world green again. Our ancestors worshiped evergreens with candles, in hopes that they could entice the sun to return. Maybe because it worked so well we've continued this tradition to the present day when we wrap tiny festive lights around boughs of spruce and pine, and sprigs of holly, mistletoe, and boxwood for holiday decorations. Candles also play an important role in another major winter holiday— the Jewish celebration of Hanukkah, the Festival of Lights. It is no wonder that the menorah, a special nine-branch candelabrum that symbolizes the Jewish holiday season, resembles a lighted tree.

For those of us who choose to continue the Christmas tree tradition, finding the perfect one can be a bit of a challenge. Artificial and fresh Christmas trees come in all sizes, shapes, and varieties. If you want to buy a fresh tree, here are some suggestions. Remember most trees sold in nurseries are cut several weeks before they are sold. Test the needles first to see if they come off when you pull them. If they do, it means the tree has already started to dry out. Unless you're keeping it up for only a few days, find another one. Dry trees are a serious fire hazard—especially if, like us, your tree is near a fireplace. To keep the tree moist, cut the end a few inches to help it drink as soon as you get it home. Immediately put it on the stand with adequate water in the tray. Check the water level daily. Although they seem to dry out more readily than other types, Douglas firs are among the easiest to shape and trim. We always liked them because lots of ornaments can be snuggled into their numerous short, bushy limbs. With fewer branches, pines are more difficult to shape so you may be stuck with the basic form of the tree you come home with. Of all the pines, the short-needled Scotch pine is a beautiful, easy-to-trim tree that is reasonably priced. Nothing can beat the aroma of the balsam fir, but it is among the most expensive of trees. Despite all the tugging and snipping, when the last ornament is hung and the lights are finally plugged in, each tree is filled with the magic of Christmas.

> O Christmas Tree, O Christmas Tree,
> Thy beauty is entrancing:
> At Christmastime, aglow with light,
> Thy presence fills us with delight!
> —seventeenth-century German folk song

Decorations from Nature

> Out in the garden stood a stately snow maiden, crowned with holly, bearing a basket of fruit and flowers in one hand, a great roll of new music in the other, a perfect rainbow of an afghan around her chilly shoulders, and a Christmas carol issuing from her lips. . . .
> —Louisa May Alcott, *Little Women*

Holiday decorations from nature have a special warmth that just can't be replicated with manufactured ornaments. Fruits, nuts, berries, holly and pine sprays, and pine cones are all beautiful raw materials for wreaths, tree ornaments, mantel sprays, evergreen ropes, and table centerpieces. When they are supplemented with paperwhites, poinsettias, cyclamen, and Christmas cactus, the entire house is transformed into a garden. Here are some of my favorites that I use year after year.

RECYCLING THE AUTUMN

Indian corn from autumn centerpieces can be reused as tree decorations. Clip the dried purple husks from the corn and place them on the tree horizontally. They look like ribbons.

THE MIDAS TOUCH

I don't know how I would decorate for the holidays without gold paint. It's versatile, easy to use, and lasts from year to year. Last year I finally finished a gallon can I've had for at least four years! Pomegranates dried and highlighted with gold paint to allow the delicate mauve to show through the gold make wonderful ornaments. They are extremely hard, though, and must be drilled in order to insert a wire hanger. Likewise, pine cones, walnuts, and cinnamon sticks can be dipped or touched up with gold paint and used on wreaths or centerpieces. These all will last from one year to the next. Amazingly enough, gold paint even adheres to plastic flowerpots. The ordinary plastic containers amaryllis and poinsettias are grown in just do not fit in with my idea of holiday decorations. An easy alternative to transplanting is to paint the original plastic pot with gold paint. Then, the pot lives up to the grandeur of its occupant.

HOLIDAY COLORS

For a spectacularly festive centerpiece, start with a clear glass punch or salad bowl centered on a round glass tray several inches larger than the bowl. Fill the bowl with a colorful cranberry salad or strawberry dessert. Around the base of the tray alternate sprigs of holly with the tiny tangerines called clementines available during the holidays.

WALL SPRAY

One of the best things about having a fresh tree is the mounds of left-over evergreen that can be used for decorations. To make a wall spray, dip six or eight pieces of dried allium in gold paint. Use florist wire to secure the allium to the base of several branches of evergreen. Wrap the wire and the end of the "bouquet" with a pretty gold ribbon and bring it up to finish in a beautiful bow, allowing the ends to drape down. Tie a piece of the wire in the evergreen to make a wall hook.

Gifts from the Garden

Few gifts are as personal and thoughtful as those from your own garden. What could be more meaningful than to transform the flowers and herbs you have grown into beautiful and useful treasures for your friends, who are sure to appreciate your sharing this special part of your life with them. Here is a sampling of some of the gifts that have been hits with my friends and family.

At Christmas I no more desire a rose
Than wish a snow in May's newfangled mirth;
But like of each thing that in season grows.
—Shakespeare, *Love's Labor's Lost*

FOR ANOTHER GARDENER

During the growing season take pictures of flowers at their peak. When the flower goes to seed, collect the seeds and save them along with the photo. Make a notecard using an attractive heavyweight paper found in art supply stores. Using a razor and ruler, cut the paper at least two inches larger than the photo on all sides and double it so it can be folded in half. Fold the paper and center the photo on the front of one half and paste it in place. To frame the photo, cut a two-inch mat from another piece of paper so that the outside edge of the mat is even with the edge of the front of the notecard. Glue the mat in place. Fill a tiny envelope such as those used for "thank-you" notes with the seeds. Write the flower's common and Latin names, when and where you collected the seed, and planting information on the envelope, and glue it inside the card. Add an appropriate poem or thought on the card. Your friend will enjoy this gift all summer long.

GIVING SWEET DREAMS

Lavender has long been used as a soothing herb to alleviate lovesickness, headaches, and a variety of other ailments. Its wonderful aroma and therapeutic properties have made it the main ingredient in sachets for linens and lingerie since the Romans. More recently lavender pillows were a favorite remedy used by Victorian ladies to soothe a wide variety of body pains and heartaches. I grow several kinds of lavender as well as another aromatic herb recommended for headaches, lemon verbena. Both are perfect for herbal pillows—a guarantee for sweet dreams. Rather than making decorative pillows that won't take the wear and tear of real use, I like to make a real bed pillow with an herbal packet inserted in the middle. To make the herbal packet, sew a ten-inch square of muslin or silk on three sides, leaving the two side seams open two inches at the top. Hem both sides of the top. Fill to halfway with equal amounts of dried and crushed lavender and lemon verbena. Then, bring one side over the other, making a flap. Secure the outside flap with hooks and eyes. Make a standard-sized pillow—about nineteen by twenty-four inches—out of a pretty white or natural cotton fabric and stuff it with cotton batting. Insert the herbal packet in the batting close to the surface as you stuff the pillow. Be careful not to bury the herbs so deeply that you can't smell them! Use a zipper or an easily removed hand stitch on one end of the cover so you can open the pillow and replenish the herbs periodically. Take care not to over-stuff the pillow; it's better for your neck. You might want to enclose a set of pillowcases edged with lavender lace so your friend understands that this pillow should be used like any other bed pillow.

Greeting Spring with a Ribbon Card

This is a variation on a Victorian Christmas decoration that used Christmas cards hung on a red or green velvet ribbon. During the summer press small (two to three inches) sprays of various flowers like baby's breath or lavender or individual blossoms such as violets, pansies, or rosebuds by placing them between sheets of wax paper in a heavy book. Place the book on its side and weigh it down with bricks on top. When the flowers have thoroughly dried, use tweezers to attach each to the front of a plain five-by-seven notecard using a hot glue gun. Cover the front with transparent rice paper and mat with an attractive heavy-weight paper with a rough edge to frame the flower. You'll need three to four cards to make one ribbon card. Try to use different flowers on each.

To finish the ribbon card, iron one yard of heavy silk ribbon in a spring color compatible with your flowers and mat. My favorite ribbon is a French silk muted stripe in light green and apricot. Finish the ribbon by carefully cutting the end in an inverted *V.* Glue three or four of the pressed flower cards at regular intervals on the ribbon. Make a beautiful bow with an additional two feet of ribbon and glue it to the top of the ribbon with the cards attached. All you need now is a hook for hanging your ribbon card on the wall, which you can easily make by looping a piece of florist wire through the back of the bow. A florist box used for long-stemmed roses is a wonderful way to present the ribbon card to your friend.

Merry Berry Holiday Pie

Cranberries just say holiday to me! I try to use them in as many different ways as I can. This pie is as festive as it is delicious.

Peel and slice two Bartlett pears into a bowl. Push three cups of fresh, washed, and drained cranberries through a food grinder with a medium disk. Do not use a food processor. If you don't have a food grinder, chop by hand until the cranberries are in small pieces. Add the cranberries to the pears with a half cup of orange marmalade and one and two-thirds cups of sugar and mix. If desired, mix in three-quarters cup of chopped walnuts. Pour into an unbaked nine-inch pie shell. Lattice-weave the top and bake in a preheated oven at 375 degrees for an hour or until the top has browned. Cool before serving so the juices jell somewhat.

Keepsake Tree Ornaments

All green was vanished save of pine and yew,
That still displayed their melancholy hue;
Save the green holly with its berries red,
And the green moss that o'er the gravel spread.
                                    —George Crabbe

Tree ornaments are special keepsakes. Reminiscing about when and where we accumulated certain ornaments is one of the many things that makes decorating the tree a warm and happy event. A few years ago I realized that tree ornaments could easily be made if I followed a method similar to that used for ball topiaries. These aromatic decorations—many from the garden—will make your tree completely unique. Most will keep for several years if you wrap them individually in bubble wrap before you store them. Next year you may want to add a few new items to refresh the scent.

Start with Styrofoam balls readily available in craft stores. The typical size for ornaments is two inches, but you can use any size. If you use larger balls, consider the total weight of the items you apply so they don't become too heavy! Stick a pencil in the top of the ball to use as a holder. Using a glue gun, squiggle hot glue over the entire ball, one half at a time. Roll the ball in sheet moss to cover. Press until the moss is secure. Decorate the ball with any of the following: cloves, dried rosebuds, slices of dried apples, small slivers of dried orange rind, dried rosemary, nuts dipped in gold paint, or tiny pine cones. Cloves can be stuck in, but all other items should be attached individually with a dab of glue and pressed tight. Although you can mix and match, try covering some balls entirely with one item.

Other types of ornaments can be made by spreading the entire ball with glue and rolling it in potpourri or lavender. This is especially nice with some of the special evergreen-scented Christmas potpourri. You can also try individually gluing holly leaves with berries to cover the entire ball.

To make a hanger, cut a ten-inch piece of narrow, strong ribbon. Remove the pencil and stick some glue in the hole. Poke the ribbon in the hole with the pencil and hold until it's secure. Cut the ribbon to the desired length and tie the ornament to the tree.

11
Winter Beauty

My garden is a forest ledge
  Which older forests bound;
The banks slope down to the blue lake-edge,
  Then plunge to depths profound.
     —Ralph Waldo Emerson, "My Garden"

Winter beauty is more subtle than the riot of spring bulbs or summer flowers—especially when there's no snow to mask the bare earth and gracefully outline the trees. When Michael and I lived in upstate New York we discovered the unexpected beauty of winter in the Catskill Mountains. On bleak January and February weekends we explored the haunting stillness of Minnewaska, Mohonk, and other forests in the magical Shawangunks—the ancient chain of rocky ridges that surrounded our house. Although the higher altitudes were covered with snow much of the winter, the lower trails were often clear and remarkably friendly. We were alone with nature when she was the most exposed. Trees were transformed into massive sculptures with a power hidden by summer foliage. We welcomed the sight of gleaming white birches in the distance, evergreen blankets of mountain laurel, and the red flashes of hawthorn berries. Virgin pines protected outcroppings of blue stone and gave us a dry place to rest and observe the silent beauty around us. These sights opened my eyes to the majesty of winter and encouraged me to give it the respect it deserved in my own garden.

Now, when it's three below zero and the pipes in the upstairs bathroom are frozen, the muted, pewter shades and solid forms of my garden are strangely pleasing and restful. A decorative kale in outlandish shades of purple and lavender still thrives in a concrete planter after being protected by the winter's heavy blanket of snow. I sneak peeks out the window at the amazing kale several times a day and thank the giant sycamore tree for keeping guard over the entire garden. I love to look at the pots and trellises I collected over the years that are no longer lost in a jumble of flowers and vines. I'm especially thrilled to see that the new wisteria arbor looks like it has always been there with one foot standing in the perennial bed and the other in the roses. The little rock path, an ancient wooden bench, and even the simple garden shed have a stark dignity that makes them surprisingly picturesque.

Summertime distractions are gone and I can see the garden as it really is. Cheerful red berries cover the hollies. Hundred-year-old honey locusts have such a commanding presence that they appear to be the true owners of the place. The objects that fill the garden are so much a part of the landscape that I'm convinced they've grown roots as surely as the trees. After many years of thinking of the cold months as a time to study catalogs and plan for spring, the mountains showed me how to appreciate the miracle of unmasked beauty and the mark of winter in my garden.

When the snow falls,
Behold each bush and tree,
Till then fast bound by winter,
Breaks forth into such blossoms
As in spring we never see.
—traditional Japanese poem

Wisdom from
Mamaw Tribby's Garden

He thought he saw a Garden-Door
That opened with a key:
He looked again, and found it was
A Double Rule of Three:
"And all its mystery," he said,
"Is clear as day to me!"
      —Lewis Carroll, "The Mad Gardener's Song"

During the long winter afternoons when the weather kept us indoors, Mamaw Tribby used to tell the story of a selfish man and a special garden. This wonderful garden had fallen into the hands of a new owner who loved it very much but didn't want to share it with anyone. He didn't know that neighborhood children had taken care of this garden as far back as anyone could remember. After the selfish man moved in, they came to do the gardening as usual. He came running out the door—screaming at the top of his lungs, "This is my garden now. Stay out or I'll call your parents."

Spring came, then summer, and everybody else's garden flourished, but nothing bloomed in his. The man was mystified.

Finally, one day he noticed a tomato plant outside the kitchen window was covered with tiny yellow flowers. He stepped outside to admire it and, just then, he heard small voices laughing. He was so happy he forgot to yell at the children. The oldest boy stepped forward and politely asked the man if they could help him with some chores. The man was impressed and decided maybe children weren't so bad after all. The children started coming to the garden every day—just as they used to do—to hoe and water the plants that had started to bloom. Once again the garden began to thrive as if it was happy to have its family home. The man looked forward to seeing the children come bounding through the gate and was surprised to discover that they no longer annoyed him. He sent them home with tomatoes in the summer and apples in the fall. Mamaw Tribby said, "The true magic of the garden was that it taught a selfish man how to share."

Lessons from the Gardener's Journal

Winter Jasmine and Other Flowering Treats

Plants flowering in winter are almost as magical as a snow-covered garden. As a child I always thought of house plants as foliage like dieffenbachia, philodendron, rubber plant, snake plant, and aspidistra. When I began gardening, I thought of it solely as an outdoor activity without really considering the possibilities of winter flowering plants. Several years ago I started overwintering my patio and garden plants as a way to save them and have even larger specimens the next spring. Gradually I've come to savor the pleasures of having an indoor garden, but it has taken a lot of effort. Unfortunately, my house is far from ideal for house plants. Like most eighteenth-century houses, ours has a lot of character, but not much light. The addition of skylights in the kitchen and pantry allowed me to bring in the bougainvillea, allamanda, and hibiscus from the patio with space left over to display whatever else is in bloom. Over the years other small but significant changes allowed me to capture the only decent morning light we get in the bedroom and my office. My efforts paid off handsomely in exotic flowering plants ready to burst open and flood the room with living color.

The indoor garden reflects as much of a seasonal shift in blooms as does the outdoor garden. In October and November, scarlet and yellow mums and hyacinths in antique bulb vases awaken the entire house with the vivid earth colors of the autumn landscape. Next come the paperwhites. Their intensely sweet smell always causes Michael to sniff and look for the source of the strange odor. If he knew the paperwhites were the culprit, I'm afraid he might give me an ultimatum—him or these charming little reminders of spring—so I cover by making an offhanded comment about taking out the garbage. The paperwhites tide me over to the red flowers of Christmas—poinsettias, cyclamen, amaryllis, Christmas cactus. The house never looks complete without an amaryllis in bloom on Christmas Day! I finally found a cool, bright spot that the cyclamen like, and they have rewarded me with long displays of intense pink blooms. In February the winter jasmine opens its little star-shaped white flowers and floods my office with its exotic perfume. In just a few weeks pots of forced bulbs can be retrieved from the garage where they have been rooting. In addition to these special seasonal blooms, geraniums, begonias, and hibiscus bloom prolifically throughout the winter season. I'll never again endure winter without an indoor garden!

. . . when she thought of the moonflowers that grew over Mrs. Tellamantez's door, it was as if she had been that vine and had opened up in white flowers every night.

—Willa Cather, *The Song of the Lark*

Growing an Indoor Garden

1. When you bring plants indoors check carefully for insects and wipe the leaves with insecticidal soap. If you need to transplant, do so a few weeks before you bring the plant inside to give it a bit of time to adapt before you add the stress of changing its environment.

2. Regardless of how careful you are, spills from overzealous watering are inevitable. After watermarking several tabletops, I've learned to make no compromises in having large, strong saucers for each pot. Clay is the most dependable. If you use the thin plastic trays that conveniently fit inside the decorative pots, double them.

3. Invest in a small watering can with a long spout to ensure an accurate aim. Mine holds a little more than three pints—just the right amount to water four or five average-sized pots. It's light and greatly eases watering. The copper or galvanized steel models are pretty enough to leave out as a constant reminder to check water levels.

4. Identify places in the house you can situate plants. Separate according to temperature and light. Keep them out of hot and cold drafts. Although it's a good idea not to move plants too often, don't miss the opportunity to show off a flower in bloom. Mobility is one of the great benefits of an indoor garden.

5. Learn and respect your plants' quirks. Kalanchoe and tuberous begonias, for example, need breathing room. It's important not to place them too close to other plants; they need space for the air to circulate. Invariably each spring my hibiscus seems to get infected with mites. After New Year's I take special care to wash it with insecticidal soap.

6. Look at your plants daily. Flowering plants grown indoors are less forgiving than when they are outside. Pick off wilted blooms and dead leaves as they occur. Dryness leading to wilting or infestation of mites or other insects can happen in just a few days.

7. Supplement natural light with fluorescent or grow lights if, like me, you aren't blessed with lots of big windows and southern exposures.

8. Fertilize with a product especially formulated for house plants. Usually a weekly feeding or a small dose in every watering works well. Slightly increase feeding as a plant approaches blooming and decrease afterward.

Let us love winter, for it is the spring of genius.
—Pietro Aretino, letter to Agostino Ricchi, July 10, 1537

FLOWERING HOUSE PLANTS FOR CHILLY ROOMS

Cineraria: Good light but no direct sun; never overcrowd; good drainage in potting medium; use 15-30-15.

Cyclamen: Good light but no direct sun; moist soil; use 15-30-15.

Winter jasmine: Bright light, with some sun; night temperatures no higher than 50 degrees while the buds set from November to January; don't prune.

Tuberous begonia: Can tolerate filtered light; moist soil; use diluted 15-30-15.

Geranium: Sun; allow soil to dry completely before watering; use 15-30-15 frequently.

FLOWERING HOUSE PLANTS FOR WARM ROOMS

Hibiscus: Sun; water frequently; use 15-30-15.

Gardenia: Sun; evenly moist; use 30-10-10.

Amaryllis: Sun; 15-30-15; keep bulb somewhat dry until bud forms, then water freely.

Moth orchid: Bright light; use orchid fertilizer; moist to slightly dry; needs moist air.

Scarlet plume: Sun; water freely while flowering, then reduce; avoid drafts; use 15-30-15; cut back new growth after flowering.

Glouvine

> A cup of hot wine with not a drop of allaying
> Tiber in 't.
> —Shakespeare, *Coriolanus*

A cup of hot spiced wine will go a long way toward lifting your spirits this time of the year. Pour a bottle of red table wine into a saucepan. Simmer for about fifteen minutes over a low flame with two sticks of cinnamon, five whole cloves, four one-inch-wide strips of orange zest, and a third of a cup of orange-flavored liqueur. If desired, add sugar to taste. Remove the cloves and zest and serve with a cinnamon stick in each cup.

Spiced Mango Vinegar

Flavored vinegars add unusually pleasant seasonings to salads, grilled fish, and vegetables and are easy to make. This one adds a touch of magic to a midwinter meal. Wash a clear quart bottle in very hot, soapy water. Rinse the bottle well. Add one pint of luke-warm, high-quality white wine vinegar. Slice five or six slivers of a ripe mango and add to the vinegar along with five or six whole cloves. Seal tightly and let it sit on the countertop for three days, turning it occasionally. Strain the vinegar through a clean coffee filter or cheesecloth and pour into a sterilized decorative bottle. Cork tightly. Keeps for two or three months in the refrigerator. Over the years I've collected pretty antique bottles for no particular reason—I just liked them. Then, I started making vinegars and realized their lovely shapes and colors were an ideal way to store and display these tempting condiments.

12

Putting Down Roots

Part of *being* in a place is getting down into its crannies and staying there long enough to see it in small details.
—James Alexander Thom,
The Spirit of the Place: Indiana Hill Country

Winter is the time when everything is reduced to the bare essentials and many everyday distractions vanish. I've always thought of this lull in activity as nature's way of getting us to reflect and contemplate, but now it seems Michael and I really don't have a choice. We're in the middle stage of life—we call it the second puberty—and identities we once thought intractable are crumbling like the dead leaves in my flower bed. Discussions about the way we live and work have taken a more serious turn. Like all of our friends at this age, we feel in our bones the time is ripe for change but what, where, and when are still a mystery.

Last summer was an important occasion, a rite of passage of sorts—we finally completed the renovation of the house and most of the garden. The finishing touches were all exterior: redoing the brick walls and front patio, painting the outside of the house, and adding an awning to cover the back patio. These changes combined with planting more perennials and bulbs finally brought the character of the house back to how it must have been two hundred years ago. I am embarrassed to admit—as much as I have looked forward to reaching this goal—that my mind chatters with thoughts about moving on to a new challenge. Our friends and family sense that this house has become a more permanent home than the other four Michael and I have renovated, but they still tease us about whether we are getting ready to move again. I wouldn't dare tell them the truth—they already think we're crazy because we've never stuck around to enjoy the fruits of our labor. Somewhere along the way Michael observed that I must be trying to fill the void left when I moved away from the farm, and he was right.

In the last few years my longing to return to the hill country in Indiana—the place I still call home—has grown from a passing thought to an ache. In the twenty-five years I've been away, I've unconsciously sought out places with winding hills and rough, rural terrains that remind me of home, but have yet to replace it. I hoped that roots would come if we found an old house with character, and a garden with heart. We've loved, worked, and rejoiced in our six years in this agreeable place, but those Indiana hills have cradled my family for many generations. The hills fed us, at times fought us, and ultimately welcomed our dead. At this point in our life we could return to those old hills that still claim so much of my heart or stay put and say, "This is home now." In the silence of this cold and snowy winter, we talk and meditate—together and alone. Out of the silence we understand that for now we need to put down roots in our own little Hudson River garden.

> Things flourish,
> then each returns to its root.
> Returning to the root is called
> stillness:
> Stillness is called return to Life. . . .
> —Lao-tzu, *Tao-te Ching*

Wisdom from
Mamaw Tribby's Garden

Mamaw Tribby taught me that one of the greatest joys of gardening is that it offers time to be alone with one's thoughts. With eight children, a husband, a mother-in-law, and a henhouse full of chickens to care for, gardening was her only opportunity for solitude. In addition to her beloved flowers she grew most of the family's food. Gardening for her was not only productive but a chance to do something that gave her pleasure. As she gardened, a verse would take root in her mind—a word or phrase or thought that would turn out to be the beginning of a poem. Writing was the only thing she ever truly did for herself and only because she couldn't imagine life without it. She said that sometimes it seemed like poems flourished better than flowers in her garden.

Later, as an old woman, she was left alone with only the companionship of her grandchildren and her garden. In the winter she sat in her rocking chair in front of the window in the living room looking out at her frozen roses and bare flower beds. When I asked her once what she was doing, she said, "Why, listening to my garden. Even from here its silence lets you hear the voice of God."

> Did I take time out to laugh, to love,
> To think, to see, to pray?
> These are the thoughts that cross
> my mind at the closing of the day.
> —Mamaw Tribby

Lessons
from the
Gardener's Journal

Creating a Winter Garden

> The snow whispers about me,
> And my wooden clogs
> Leave holes behind me in the snow.
> But no one will pass this way
> Seeking my footsteps,
> And when the temple bell rings again
> They will be covered and gone.
> —Amy Lowell, "Falling Snow"

I had gardened quite a few growing seasons before I began, in earnest, to uncover the beauty of the most challenging season of the year. Here in the Northeast, winters last at least five months—regardless of what the calendar says. After looking at many gardens and forests that possessed a tranquil winter beauty, I decided that they shared a simple grace mine lacked. In these winter sanctuaries, color, texture, and a sense of drama all came together effortlessly.

Like most winter gardens, mine is usually viewed from a cozy chair in front of a window, a path leading into the house, or the snow-covered sidewalk. After several years of watching the snow blanket my garden and turning to indoor plants, I wanted to use the lessons I learned from the forests of the Catskill Mountains to let my winter garden reveal its beauty. When the camouflage provided by summer foliage and flowers vanished with the frost, the first thing I noticed was that the garden's layout was busy and haphazard. I needed to accomplish two things: to introduce more plants that retain their appeal in winter and to highlight them. Hydrangeas, with their ponderous flower heads dried on the branches, are especially useful in the winter, so I incorporated several. The wheat-colored blooms of *H. paniculata "Grandiflora"* add charm to the backyard—one at its entrance and another in the border next to a red-twigged dogwood. Another hydrangea, this time a blue lace cap, is lovely in a corner of the yard. An amazing eight-foot juniper topiary tree I found at an "end-of-season" sale at a local nursery provides the perfect dramatic effect for the corner opposite the blue lace cap.

The next step in my evolution as a winter gardener was to take the radical step of leaving some of the dead foliage in my flower bed. Like most gardeners, I had been taught to clean up the garden in autumn. But one October as I tossed the dead stalks on the compost heap, I felt especially sad and wondered if this compulsive cleaning was really natural. I stood back and—to my delight—striking forms lurked among the dried stalks, curled leaves, and seed pods of the lingering perennials. The tall black stalks and large round heads of rudbeckia, echinacea, and bee balm were attractive and filled the bare ground with texture and interesting shapes. The sedum "Autumn Joy," which has always thrived for me, turned out to be another winter jewel. Its faded bronze was spectacular next to the pearly silver of a large artemisia. As I began to think about how a particular flower or shrub would look in winter, I discovered many choices that weathered especially well and enhanced the poor evergreens, who had been doing all the work alone. Visual height was added in the backyard with a wisteria-covered arbor—something I had wanted for years. It also linked my little rose garden with the perennial bed and created a flow across the middle of the backyard where previously it had been so disjointed. Now the glimpse I catch of my garden as I dash from the driveway into the house is almost as lovely in winter as in summer.

Out of one wintry twig,
     One bud
     One blossom's worth of warmth
At long last.
          —Ranstu, a haiku from *Haiku Harvest*

Planting for Winter

PERENNIALS WITH INTERESTING STALKS

"Autumn Joy" sedum: Tall, large flowers that deepen from pink to reddish bronze through the autumn and winter.

Bee Balm, Echinacea, Physostegia, and Rudbeckia: All these hardy flowers have large seed pods that remain standing on strong stalks throughout the winter.

Honesty: A biennial with interesting, almost translucent seed pods.

SHRUBS

Blazeaway heather: Beautiful all year long, but turns a warm red in winter.

Firethorn: Bright orange-red berries in late autumn best trained against a fence or wall. "Chadwickii," "Kasan," and "Lalandei" are good cold-hardy choices.

Guelder rose: In autumn the foliage turns a deep red and bountiful cranberry-like clusters appear. Cold hardy.

Japanese pieris (pink- or red-budded forms): Long, lustrous dark green leaves with red or pink winter flower buds; acid-loving and hardy.

Longstalk holly: Long green leaves with red berries; cold and wind hardy.

Oak-leafed hydrangea: Ten-inch-long creamy linen flowers bloom from midsummer through autumn and look beautiful all winter with an interesting peeling bark.

Pussy willows: Fluffy gray catkins on the female, with gold stamens on those of the male.

Witch hazel: One of the earliest flowering shrubs, often displaying scented yellow and reddish flowers around New Year's.

TREES

Birches: The gleaming straight Whitespire and the river birch with showy, peeling bark are the best.

Dogwoods: Red and yellow-twigged cultivars are especially beautiful in the winter, but the Kousa has an interesting flaking bark after it ages.

Hawthorns: Many varieties with bright red berries.

Maples: Most popular in winter is the paperbark with a dramatic peeling surface.

Cherishing Ornaments and Fixtures

'Tis an old dial, dark with many a stain;
   In summer crowned with drifting orchard bloom,
Tricked in the autumn with the yellow rain,
   And white in winter like a marble tomb.
   —Henry Austin Dobson, "The Sundial"

Last winter I saw bare wisteria vines climbing up the column of a pergola in a neighbor's garden and was reminded once again how much the right ornaments and fixtures enhance a garden. The column was so perfectly united with the wisteria it was almost as if they were one.

Isn't this the ultimate test of any object in the garden? We catch a glimpse of a scene and think, "What an appealing place!" Not, "What a charming birdbath!" Winter's sparsity gives a special prominence to permanent fixtures like fountains, birdhouses, gazebos, arbors, gates, and fences. It requires a discerning eye and an open mind to get the most out of the fixtures we've chosen, and it's often helpful to ask ourselves these questions: Does this still work here? Is it too dominant? Has it gone from being pleasantly worn to decrepit? Almost all of the things in my garden come with thoughts of special times and old friends—the decorative concrete flowerpots I've collected at flea markets, the trellis we built for the roses and the sweet peas, the tall, curved church bench we discovered at a Connecticut garage sale one sweltering July weekend, the small stone pineapple sculpture we found while visiting friends in New Jersey. When I see my history in the things surrounding me, I begin to feel as if I have something of myself in this place.

Getting Pleasure from Your Garden Treasures

Leave anything that can withstand the weather—treated wood, iron, concrete—out during the winter when they will be most appreciated and will have the most impact.

Modify outdoor lighting to highlight the special features of the winter garden.

Add interesting vine wreaths, bittersweet, or other natural touches to decorate bare objects such as a trellis, sculpture, or fountain.

Paint surfaces like the door to your garden shed or trellis to add splashes of color to the landscape.

Tummy-Warming Tomato and Herb Soup

Even though I spend less time outside in late winter than any other season, there is no escaping the damp cold that creeps inside and permeates the house. Nothing else chases away chills and warms the body and soul like a big bowl of hearty soup. I've been making this wonderful tomato and herb soup for over twenty years—usually in February when the weather gets especially cold.

Wash two short ribs of beef and place in three quarts of cold water. Cook over a medium flame and scoop off the foam as the ribs boil. Add one teaspoon of salt and a quarter teaspoon of black pepper. Let boil gently for about an hour. Add a medium carrot cut into chunks, a small chopped onion, a medium bunch of fresh parsley, chopped, and a two-pound three-ounce can of whole Italian tomatoes. Grind two teaspoons of dried rosemary from last summer's garden in a mortar and pestle and add to the soup. Continue cooking over a low flame until the meat is tender.

Put a pint of sour cream in a quart saucepan and add one tablespoon of flour, stirring to dissolve the lumps. Cook over a very low flame until the sour cream is smooth. Add a pint of the hot soup and stir well. Pour the sour cream mixture into the soup and stir. Continue cooking until it boils. Remove the bones. Serve over cooked basmati rice.

The man around the corner keeps experimenting with new flowers every year, and now has quite an extensive list of things he can't grow.
—William Vaughn, b. 1577, American colonialist

Your Gardening Journal

One season in the garden has ended, another is beginning, and a wonderful way to prepare for it is by making your own gardening journal. I was influenced by Mamaw Tribby, who kept homemade journals and notebooks her entire life. Many journals are available in gift shops, but they seem too precious to me to use as a working record of what I do in the garden. A homemade journal gives you the freedom to experiment, erase, and make it completely, uniquely your own. The journal is a personal record of a year in your garden.

To make a journal like Mamaw Tribby's, start with an inexpensive, old-fashioned scrapbook made from plain, heavy paper. Sometimes she made the book herself by binding paper with the strong thread she used in making rag rugs and using cardboard for the cover, but this is a little too rustic for me. Find a magazine photograph you love or a blown-up snapshot of your own garden and paste it on the cover. Think of a name for your journal and write it with an indelible marker on the front. You will soon find that your journal has become a valuable record of your important activities—like what you planted and when, and when you fertilized, as well as what you tried that didn't work. As time passes it will mean more to you if you note the little observations about life, the joys and frustrations that come up so frequently in the garden. I like to paste gardening ideas from the newspaper, plantings I want to replicate someday, my monthly photographs, as well as photos of other people's gardens. Keeping a colorful visual journal of your own will make planting, designing, and color-coordinating your garden easier and more creative with each passing season. In the process you may discover—as I have—that the garden is also teaching you about life.

In the end, there is really nothing more important than taking care of the earth and letting it take care of you.

—Charles Scott

Index